THE GREEK ISLANDS

Robin Mead

B. T. Batsford Ltd *London*

For Eleni, who opened my eyes to the islands

First published 1979
© Robin Mead 1979
ISBN 0 7134 0625 9 ✓

Photoset, printed and bound in Great Britain by
REDWOOD BURN LTD. Trowbridge and Esher
for the publishers
B. T. Batsford Ltd, 4 Fitzhardinge Street, London W1H 0AH

CONTENTS

LIST OF ILLUSTRATIONS

(Pages 65–80)

LIST OF MAPS

ACKNOWLEDGMENT

My thanks are due to the National Tourist Organization of Greece, both in Athens and London, for its help and hospitality while I was researching parts of this book. In particular, I am grateful to the Director of the Greek Tourist Office in London, Peter Analytis, and to his former deputy Miss Cleo Angelopoulou, now based in Athens, for their assistance and encouragement. Vital information and facilities were also provided by British Airways, Owners' Services Ltd, Olympic Holidays, Astir Hotels and Chandris Hotels, and by the following individuals: Robin Bean, Sarah Birdsey, Spyros Catechis, Peter Chambers, Jenny Crayford, Diane Crosse, Peter Drew, John Economou, Kaye Economou, Reg Fryer, George Harris, Joy Holmes, Basil Iatrides, Andrew James, Spyros Lemis, Felicity Lowe, Spyros Lychnos, Kevin McCoy, Basil Mantzos, Donald Miller, Mario Modiano, Sia Moraitou, Kelvin Moyses, Helen Nakou, Katie Pirounakis, Peter Roberts, Ron Scobling, Maggie Southam, Polly Spentza, Paula Tebbs, John Tranakas, Maureen Walker, Valerie Webster, Michael Xenakis and Aspasia Zaza. And finally my thanks must go to my wife, Marion, who uncomplainingly doubles as an unpaid secretary.

The author and publishers would like to thank the following for kind permission to reproduce their photographs: Douglas Dickens for 4, 17 and 22; A. F. Kersting for 25, 26 and 27; and Reno Wideson for 2, 7, 9, 12 and 15. Numbers 5, 8 and 11 are from the author's own collection.

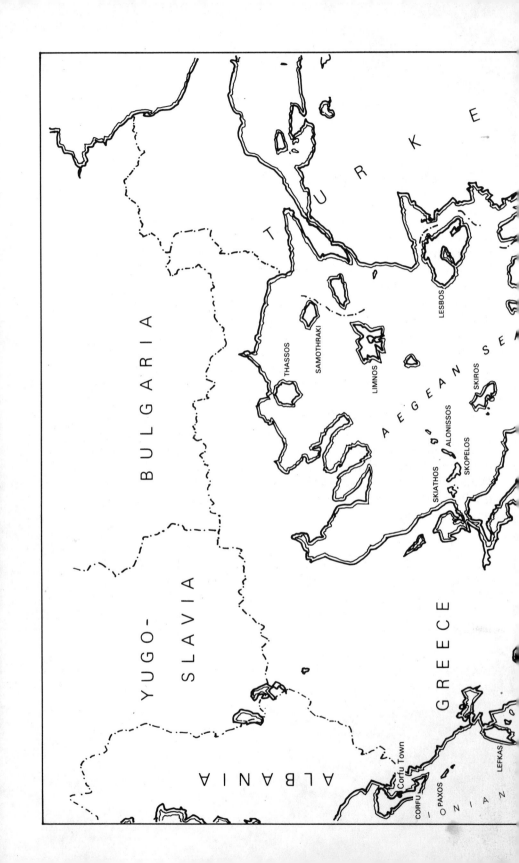

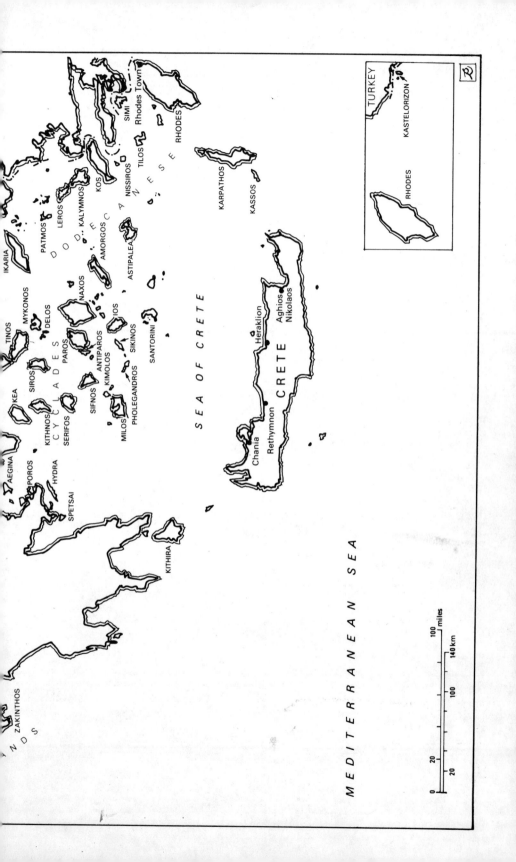

1 HISTORY AND CHARACTER

There are, at a rough count, 1,500 Greek islands—ranging from the massive, 150-mile-long bulk of mountainous Crete down to islets that are little more than rocks sticking out of the sea. They include the popular holiday islands of Corfu, Rhodes and Mykonos, which are visited by millions of tourists every year, while at the other end of the scale there are little-known islands inhabited only by fisherfolk and almost impossible to reach unless you are prepared to hire a Greek sailing-boat—a *caique*.

Together, the islands give Greece by far the longest coastline in Europe—19,600 miles of it. Individually they are all different, and perhaps this is the root of their popularity as holiday destinations. On a Greek island you can enjoy the most modern hotels and a sophisticated night-life, or you can wander at will until you find your 'own' island, where the traditions of Greek hospitality will ensure you a bed in a private house if the *taverna* is full, and where a delicious meal of fish, bread and wine will still cost you only a few pence even in these days of inflation.

But while they are all different the islands do have one thing in common: sunshine which lasts almost the whole year round. Even in the north of the country the islands lay claim to long summers and mild winters, and the traveller in November or March may find that he is enjoying shirtsleeve and swimming weather as pleasant as a summer's day. Hardly surprising, perhaps, for Crete and Rhodes are the most southerly islands in Europe, and on a latitude that puts even Tunis to the north of them.

The Ancient Greeks called the Mediterranean 'the road', and although the mountainous interior of the mainland is very much a part of modern Greece, just as the sprawling cities are, it is towards the islands littered across the blue waters of the Aegean that the face of Greece is turned. History has decreed it thus, for across these waters have come both conquerors and trading wealth, and from these islands have come many of the most famous Greeks, from

Homer down to the millionaire shipowners whose lives and loves are of such perennial interest to newspaper gossip-columnists. Sooner or later almost every Greek you meet will tell you proudly of 'my island'—the island on which his family's roots are embedded.

The islands fall into a number of main groups whose names are, to begin with, difficult to disentangle but which soon stick in the mind because of the logical groupings.

First, in the Ionian Sea off the west coast of Greece, are the Ionian islands of which Corfu is the best known. Because they are so close to Italy, and because historically they have been at the crossroads of Europe and have been occupied more times than they care to remember, these islands are more western, and more sophisticated, than any of the other Greek islands. Here west and east meet and happily intermingle. Although Corfu has built up a huge tourist industry, based very largely on holidaymakers from Britain and, to a lesser extent, from Italy, it has not done so at the cost of spoiling the island or its people—a fact that I believe contributes very largely to Corfu's popularity. The other Ionian islands, strung down the coast, see far fewer tourists and are particularly hospitable as well as retaining a greenness unusual in Greece. Many of the people are fair skinned and blue eyed—another rarity in Greece, although the original Greeks are supposed to have had that colouring. The Ionian islanders, however, owe these physical attributes to western European blood rather than to any long-lost heritage.

On the other side of the Peloponnese peninsula, the most southerly part of the Greek mainland (and, strictly speaking, itself an island since the cutting of the Corinth Canal), lie the islands closest to Athens: the Saronic isles. They owe their name to the fact that they are situated in the Saronic Gulf, and they are all within easy reach of the Greek capital. Popular with yachtsmen and day-trippers alike, they have remained remarkably unspoilt. They are mostly small, and—excepting Spetsai—they are places to visit rather than stay in.

The Cyclades were christened 'the wheeling ones' by the Ancient Greeks because they are a roughly circular group of islands that appear to wheel around the central island of Delos, which was an important religious centre. Mykonos is the most famous of this group, but because these Aegean islands have become so popular with ferry-hopping tourists who explore them without adhering to any particular holiday timetable, many other islands in this beautiful group are becoming better known and must increasingly be considered as holiday destinations in their own right.

To the north of the Cyclades, still in the Aegean, are the roughly grouped islands of the northern Aegean and the Sporades. Neither of these groups has the corporate identity of the other main groups, and neither is yet seen as a holiday area. But places like Skiathos, Thassos, Lesbos and Chios have their devotees.

Far to the south, Crete stands on its own. But close by, off the coast of Turkey, are Rhodes and the other islands of the Dodecanese group—again a largely unspoilt group visited, except for Rhodes, by only a handful of hardy holidaymakers who do not expect too much in the way of food and accommodation. The political antagonism between Greece and Turkey, which puts the Dodecanese in the front line of any conflict, and the relative infrequency of sea or air communications with Athens, have combined to keep this area in the tourism background; but once again they are opening up as more and more travellers discover them.

Despite the geographical facts, the first-time visitor may be surprised to find that the Greek islanders are not an insular people. True, the villager you meet on some remote spot in the Cyclades may never have travelled farther than the next island, or perhaps—just once—to Athens. But he or she will be well informed on everything from the country's contorted politics to the latest fashions in clothes and *bouzouki*-style pop music.

The visitor still is seen partly as a means of adding to that store of information, for Greece is only now emerging from the centuries of historical isolation and foreign domination which have encouraged people to include this essentially western nation into the boundless and mysterious world we term the Orient. No doubt the increase in tourism, and links with the European Economic Community, will speed up and complete the process, but for the present Greeks still greet tourists with a unique mixture of friendship and curiosity. Where do you come from? What do British people think of the problems between Greece and NATO? Are you married? Where did you buy your trousers? How much were they? Would you like to see a photograph of my family? Do you like my island? Those are the lines that a chance conversation with a Greek often takes—and it is often followed up with an invitation to a meal, a party, or perhaps even some local celebration such as a wedding. Greek hospitality, especially on the more remote islands, is overwhelming and can be embarrassing. Admire something—an ornament, a picture, an item of clothing—in a house in an island village and you may well find the relevant item being pressed upon you as a gift. Offer to pay, and your new friendship will come to an abrupt end.

The Mediterranean is indeed 'the road' to and between these islands, a road as picturesque as it is rich in history. Surely one of the most beautiful sights in Europe must be the green and brown patchwork quilt of the Cyclades, set in a deep blue sea, seen from the window of an aircraft crossing from Athens to Rhodes; or a Cretan sunset turning the waters of the Gulf of Mirabello into the 'wine dark sea' that Homer described.

I have often taken my family to Greece on the car ferry that runs between Brindisi, on the heel of Italy, and the Greek port of Patras. Going east, the ship crosses the Adriatic during the hours of darkness then spends the day running south past the Ionian islands, in what is as lovely a ferry-trip as you will find anywhere. My young sons have long been convinced that as the ship approaches Greece the sea turns bluer. A childish fantasy? Perhaps—but it is suggested by many experts that the waters of the eastern Mediterranean are lacking in some of the minute plants and other life forms on which small fish feed and which give more westerly waters their greenish tinge. Whether the explanation of Greece's blue seas is scientific, the work of one's imagination, or merely a reflection of cloudless summer skies, there is another, harsher, aspect to this optical delight: these are seas in which it is hard for the fishermen of the Aegean to make a living.

These shortages are not apparent in the island *tavernas*, where fish dishes feature strongly among the snacks, or *mezethes*, which Greeks take with their evening *ouzo*—the cheap, colourless local spirit that turns cloudy when water is added, tastes of aniseed, and carries an unexpected kick. Don't miss, for example, the delicious *barbounia*, or red mullet, fried and eaten whole, the *taramosalata* (fish roe) dips, or even the slices of slightly rubbery squid.

Tavernas—an individualistic mixture of restaurant, bar, and palace of varieties—are where the Greeks like to spend their evenings. The day starts early, is broken up by an afternoon siesta and, especially in the islands, finishes late. If they do not go to the *taverna*, Greeks usually spend the evening with their families, for Greece is a country where family ties are still very strong. Being invited into a Greek home is a great honour—but young tourists should beware, for being asked home by a member of the opposite sex to meet his or her family is looked upon by the older generation as notice of an impending engagement, and such an 'engagement' could prove difficult to break.

At weekends or on public holidays the gregarious Greeks head en masse for the sea, to swim and sunbathe (one of the best ways of finding a good beach on any Greek island is to follow the locals) or simply to gaze towards those distant horizons where Odysseus may have wandered and from which Greece seems to draw the very breath of life.

If Greece draws life from the sea, then our western civilization is said to owe its origins to Greece which, despite its distinctly undemocratic post-war history until recently, is described by historians as the birthplace of democracy. Certainly democracy, or a version of it, had a part to play in the development of the city-state of Athens; but that apart, Ancient Greek history is a saga of legendary feuds and wars in which fact and fiction have become inextricably intermingled. Knowledge of the flourishing and influential civilizations of Crete goes back 5,000 years to 3000 B.C. and is now based upon archaeological evidence that exists in profusion even after its meaning is questioned by various theorists. Greek civilization emerges at about 1300 B.C., and the poems of the blind Homer, dating from the end of the eighth century or the seventh century B.C., tell of the bloodthirsty struggles between the Acheans of Greece and the Phrygians of Troy between 1194 and 1184 B.C. a story considered mythical until the German archaeologist Schliemann actually unearthed the foundations of Troy and Mycenae.

Just as the stories of Robin Hood have become a part of English folklore, so the old stories of the Creation, the battles between the gods on Mount Olympus, the heroic deeds of Hercules (or, to give him his Greek name, Heracles) and the Trojan War were passed on from mouth to mouth and from generation to generation, and even partly recorded in the ancient and only recently deciphered Linear-B manuscript. This rich store of legend was known as the 'epic cycle', and it was much drawn upon by Homer as well as by later poets and dramatists. By recording these epics in composite form, Homer was unwittingly presenting historians of the future with a picture of contemporary Greek values as well as beliefs. Furthermore, he was laying the foundations of the classicism from which the writers and artists of the Renaissance—among them Botticelli,

Rubens and Shakespeare—were to draw inspiration.

Greek myths and legends are a complex mixture of religious beliefs, folk tales, fables and traditional stories that, like the tales of Troy, were based on fact. The dividing line is not always clear.

The earliest, the Olympic Creation myths, bear a certain similarity to the biblical stories of the Creation, with the Earth springing from an empty space known as Chaos and then giving birth to Uranus (the heavens) and Pontus (the sea). The events that followed, according to the myths, are rather less biblical. Uranus fathered (and the Earth, or Ge, mothered) such unlovable creatures as the hundred-handed giants called the Centimani, the one-eyed Cyclopes, and the twelve Titans. It was not a happy family: Uranus was wounded and deposed by Cronus, the youngest of the Titans, who then married his sister Rhea but swallowed each of their children at birth in order that he should not in turn be deposed by his own son. Only Zeus, the youngest, escaped this gruesome fate because Rhea gave Cronus a stone to swallow instead and hid Zeus in the Dictaean Cave on Crete. There, according to Minoan tradition, Zeus was nursed by a goat, grew to adulthood, and was eventually able to force Cronus to disgorge his brothers and sisters. Joined by his brothers, Hades and Poseidon, Zeus then waged a ten-year war against Cronus and the other Titans, led by Atlas. Plots were followed by counter-plots, and the weapons brought into play included such fearsome innovations as Zeus's thunderbolt, but the trio eventually vanquished the Titans and sentenced Atlas to carry the sky (and not the earth, as is wrongly depicted in so many cartoons) on his shoulders as a perpetual punishment. The brothers then shared out the world, with Hades taking charge of the underworld, Poseidon taking the sea, and Zeus setting up residence in the traditional spot on the summit of Mount Olympus, in northern Greece, and ruling over the sky. On Mount Olympus Zeus was joined by the eleven other Olympian deities: Poseidon; Hestia, goddess of the hearth fire; Demeter, goddess of agriculture; Hera, wife to Zeus; Aphrodite, the goddess of desire known to the Romans as Venus; Pallas Athene, who embodied wisdom and power; Apollo the god of the sun; Artemis the huntress; Hephaestus, the smith god; Ares, god of war; and Hermes. Later a newcomer, Dionysus, the wine god, was to take the place of Hestia.

The deeds of each of the Olympian deities, the story of Jason and the Argonauts, the labours of Heracles, the history of the Trojan

War, the separate Cretan and Theban myths, and the wanderings of Odysseus—all are told in the ancient legends. But besides forming the basis of the people's religious beliefs and relating what was supposed to be the history of the eastern Mediterranean world, the legends also served to explain some of the natural phenomena of the time and the area. The smoke and flames pouring from volcanic Mount Etna in Sicily, for example, was said to be due to the burial beneath the mountain of either Enceladus or Typhon, one of the enemies of Zeus.

The creation of mankind was ascribed in the legends to one of the Titans, Prometheus. Zeus, in what one may now regard as a genuine flash of divine intuition about the future misdeeds of Prometheus's creation, was sufficiently enraged to chain Prometheus to a crag in the Caucasus and instruct an eagle to tear at his liver all day long—a punishment the unfortunate Prometheus was to endure for many years until Heracles finally shot the eagle. Soon after this point in the legends the similarity with the Old Testament stories reappears, for it was said that Zeus decided to wipe out mankind with a flood. But Prometheus's son, Deucalion, as independent and as inventive as his father, saved his family by building an ark and riding out the nine-day flood until the ark finally came to rest on Mount Parnassus. Deucalion's son, Hellen, is the mythical ancestor of all the Hellenic people.

Archaeologists give the Hellenes a rather more prosaic background. As a people they are thought to be a northern, Aryan race, equipped with horses and wheeled vehicles, who moved into mainland Greece in the Middle Bronze Age, at about 2000 b.c., and fused with the Mediterranean stock who had spread into the country a thousand years earlier and had replaced the indigenous Neolithic people.

The Mediterranean peoples had long enjoyed a civilization of their own centred upon the Cyclades islands. The Aegean is largely cut off from the rest of the Mediterranean; it is in effect an island-studded lake bounded to the north and west by the Greek mainland, to the east by Turkey, and to the south by mountainous Crete. The Levantine people who had settled on Crete as early as 5000 b.c. built up in the Cyclades a peaceful trading community, for sea travel was comparatively simple and in those waters a sailor was seldom out of sight of land. Relatively prosperous, and apparently without enemies, the Cretans built extensive and unfortified settlements at

Knossos, near the present capital of the island, Heraklion, and at Phaistos in the south. In the Cyclades the islanders turned industriously to mining, and traded in copper and gems. Mariners ventured to Asia and Africa to find the tin with which copper must be combined to make bronze.

The Minoan civilization at Knossos is named after the legendary King Minos of Crete, whose horrific bull-headed son, the Minotaur, was reputed to be kept in a labyrinth of passages through which the Athenian prince Theseus was able to find his way and kill the Minotaur only by using a reel of thread in order to be able to retrace his steps. When the archaeologist Sir Arthur Evans excavated Knossos in 1900 the ruins that he found were so extensive that he thought at first he had discovered the legendary labyrinth, and that another of the old stories had come true. In fact, he was in the luxurious palace of Knossos, built in a style centuries ahead of its time. Light-wells let in the sunshine, there were efficient washing and toilet facilities, and the cellars were found to be stuffed with jars of food and wine.

Those were the days of wine and roses in the Aegean. Painting, sculpture, sport—such were the pastimes of a people who had both the leisure and the wealth to indulge themselves. That, at least, is the theory propounded by Evans—and still the one adhered to by most archaeologists. But the German geologist, Professor Hans Georg Wunderlich, has put forward an alternative proposition. He points to some extraordinary omissions on the part of the builders of Knossos—such as the lack of kitchens or stables among the hundreds of rooms, and the fact that the royal apartments are at a very low, dimly lit level. Wunderlich also notes that the Linear-B texts, translated after Evans's death, were in an Ancient Greek dialect, which places a big question-mark after the Evans hypothesis that the Minoan culture was essentially pre-Greek. In his book *The Secret of Crete* Wunderlich comes out in support of an earlier German critic of Sir Arthur Evans, the philosopher Oswald Spengler, who in the 1930s argued that 'the absence of any protecting wall around ancient Cretan palaces and country estates, the pictures of bulls so reminiscent of the ancient Minotaur legend and that peculiar king's throne in the Palace of Knossos, which in his view would be more suitable "for a votive image or a priest's mummy",' prompted him to ask: 'Were the "palaces" of Knossos and Phaistos temples of the dead, sanctuaries of a powerful cult of the hereafter? . . .' The question, Wunderlich says, seems worthy of serious consideration. He goes on to argue a strong Egyptian influence in Minoan Crete, and offers evidence that the palaces were indeed mausoleums to early cult figures, carrying on the heroic culture of the Ancient Greeks.

Whatever the answer to this fascinating archaeological riddle, nature was to intervene dramatically in the Aegean.

It is still not known quite what happened, or when. Perhaps this Aegean civilization was the mysterious Atlantis, and doubtless if it had been allowed to continue, the history of the entire area, and perhaps of the world, would have been very different. But, some time around 1500 B.C., a cataclysmic earthquake or volcanic eruption shattered the area. The clues are few and far between, but the Greek legend of Deucalion and the flood, the biblical story of the parting of the Red Sea, modern radio-carbon dating, and in the middle of the Aegean the visual evidence of the extraordinary sunken crater and the islets, one of them still smoking, that make up Santorini, all point to a volcanic eruption of unimaginable proportions. Indeed, Santorini still reminds one irresistably of what it in fact is: an enormous volcanic crater peeping above the waves.

Santorini is estimated to have exploded with a force three times greater than Krakatoa's, whose eruption in 1883 killed some 36,000 people in Java and Sumatra with tidal waves, and which was heard 2,000 miles away. Santorini, then known as Thira, all but disappeared; the north coast of Crete, every Aegean island, and most ports on mainland Greece must have been devastated. Few vessels in the Mediterranean could have remained afloat, and the loss of life must have been enormous. The glorious Minoan culture, which— assuming it existed—had no enemies but nature, disappeared beneath the waves or was buried under 130 feet of volcanic ash.

The heirs to the Minoan civilization were the war-like Mycenaeans from mainland Greece, named after their principal city, Mycenae, in the Peloponnese. Although the Mycenaeans inherited some aspects of Minoan culture, such as writing, they did not build great cities. True they built palaces at Mycenae itself, at Tiryns, at Pylos, and on the rock of the Acropolis in Athens. But they devoted much of their time to warfare, invasion and conquest. Syria, Cyprus and the coastline of Asia Minor all suffered the deprivations of these cruel slave-traders, and the best-known attack of all was on the city of Troy in about 1200 B.C. By this time the Greek peoples were loosely united under Mycenaean rule, and their king, Agamemnon, led the expedition against Troy from which grew one of the last, and perhaps the greatest, of the Greek legends. Twelve hundred ships, many of them from the islands, are said to have taken part in the siege of Troy, and the eventual capture of the city by means of a ruse—hiding Greek soldiers in a wooden horse presented to the Trojans—is a story we still learn as children. It is also the incident that gave rise to the popular expression which, even today, Hellenic people regard as an insult: 'Beware of Greeks bearing gifts.'

But the Trojan War, coupled with internal strife, undermined the strength of the Mycenaeans and brought their civilization to almost as abrupt an end as its predecessor. Towards the end of the twelfth century B.C. new invaders, the Dorians, a semi-barbarous people armed with iron swords, swept down from what are now Bulgaria and Yugoslavia, sacking Pylos and Tiryns and buring Mycenae. Only the Acropolis in Athens escaped the destruction. The Dorians were not interested in art, writing, architecture or even trade; they lived by conquest and destruction. The Mycenaeans withdrew to the Greek islands.

Eventually, however, invaders and invaded were to mingle and merge. The Dorians' iron tools revolutionized farming, and in places like Sparta and Corinth there were established self-supporting independent city-states that were governed by men who had the wealth or the strength to subdue and hold the surrounding area. From these city-states, adventurers once again set sail to explore and colonize the Aegean world and beyond. Settlements grew up on parts of the Black Sea coastline, in Libya, Sicily, southern Italy, and even as far afield as the coasts of France and Spain. The Italians invented a word for these settlers from the east: Greeks.

At home, things were changing fast and new ideas were developing. Religion, based upon the worship of the gods on Mount Olympus, was widespread, and the religious centres at Olympia, Delphi, and Eleusis attracted a considerable following. Writing returned to the country, although the new Greek alphabet was Phoenician, and philosophy, poetry and science all reappeared.

Athens, which was well placed geographically and was surrounded by fertile land, grew and prospered. On top of the rock of the Acropolis the Athenians had built a magnificent temple to the goddess Athene, after whom the city was named. But the grandeur of this magnificent structure disguised a simmering discontent over the gulf that had arisen between the rich farm-owners and the peasants. The only law was the one decreed by the aristocrats, and it fell to one of these aristocrats, Solon, to introduce a radical programme of reform in about 590 B.C. Solon's innovations included a 400-member governing council for the city drawn from all classes, and the establishment of courts and the jury system. Democracy had been born.

It was a short-lived reform. When Solon retired, the new schemes were quickly dropped by the aristocracy who again seized power. But the poorer classes, having had a taste of freedom, rebelled and elected their own leader, Pisistratus, in about 560 B.C., giving him the powers of *tyrant*, a Greek word meaning king in all but name. Pisistratus governed Athens well for 20 years; under his guidance the city prospered as a commercial and financial centre, money having been introduced into Greece from Asia Minor. Gold and silver were mined in Greece under Athenian guidance, and the city became the leader of the Greek city-states. Its only rival was Sparta, in the Peloponnese, where the mainly Dorian people were still poor but had all the pride and toughness of their ancestors. Sparta was the only part of Greece to create and maintain a standing army, training boys and young men to a harsh, military way of life that was truly Spartan.

After the death of Pisistratus there was a brief period of turmoil in Athens before the people elected a new leader, Cleisthenes, a political reformer who attempted to expand upon the democratic innovations of Solon and who is today credited with being the first leader to introduce democratic government. Cleisthenes introduced the principles by which every free Greek citizen could attend an assembly of the people and discuss city affairs, and a new 500-member ruling council was set up, its members being elected by the people.

Meanwhile, in the Middle East, a new power had arisen: Persia. Under the wise leadership of King Cyrus the Great, Persia had established a sphere of influence that stretched from India to Asia Minor, and the Persian policy was that these places should be granted a large measure of self-government. One of Cyrus's successors, Darius, had added to the Persian empire by conquering large areas of south-eastern Europe, including Macedonia. But at the beginning of the fifth century B.C. some Ionian cities revolted against Persian overlordship and asked Athens and the city of Eretria, on the island of Euboea, north-east of Athens, for help. Athens and Eretria sent an expeditionary force to help the rebels, and this force attacked and razed the Persian provincial capital of Sardis. It was a lone success, for the revolt was crushed and Persian anger was directed against Greece. Envoys sent to Athens and Sparta were executed and Darius, who made a servant repeat to him every night the words, 'Remember the Athenians', began to prepare an army of revenge to lay siege to Athens. The anxious Athenians asked Sparta and the other city-states for help, but they all declined. The one exception was little Plataea, which offered 1,000 men.

Darius did not go in for any half measures. His army of 40,000 men, in 600 vessels, sacked Eretria, burned its temples and carried off the entire population as prisoners, as retribution for the burning of Sardis. Darius planned to punish Athens in the same way. Only 10,000 Athenian citizen-soldiers, plus the contingent from Plataea, stood between the city and the formidable Persian force.

The Persians cannot have expected the tiny Greek army to attack, especially as it had no bowmen and the men were armed principally with spears. But attack they did, and thanks to their enthusiasm for athletics the Greeks were very fit. What is more they were desperate, and desperate men can work wonders. Unable to manoeuvre, the Persians gave ground, and a final attack by two Greek squadrons of cavalry threw the invaders into confusion. Before evening they were retreating towards their ships and the following Greeks captured seven vessels. It proved to be a memorable victory, for the Greeks lost 192 dead, against Persian losses of no less than 6,400 men. A Greek athlete, Pheidippides, was despatched to Athens, 26 miles away, to announce the victory. He ran all the way, gasped out his message, then collapsed and died—an incident still commemorated in the marathon race at today's Olympic Games.

Persia had been defeated, but a long-standing enmity had begun. Even Sparta, which regretted its part in killing one of Darius's messengers and sent two volunteers to his court to apologize and offer their lives in retribution, could not heal the breach. When they arrived Darius was dead, but his son, Xerxes, sent the messengers home with the warning that Sparta could not escape the burden of its guilt by offering Persia the chance of reprisals.

In 481 B.C., Xerxes was ready. A huge army said to number five million men, although historians are divided on this point, was marshalled at the Hellespont, the modern-day Dardanelles. When this army crossed the straits and began its march along the coastline of northern Greece, the Persian navy supported it with supplies. The Greeks, despite having had ample warning of the invasion, were unprepared because of disagreements between the city-states, but they had built a fleet of about 200 ships which assembled in Piraeus, the harbour of Athens. They also had another strong card in their hands, for this time the Spartans were on their side. Leonidas, the King of Sparta, took personal command of the Spartan troops and of the 20,000-strong Greek army. But, despite the threat of attack, it was the season for the Olympic Games in Greece, the regular sporting event during which war and fighting were considered improper. As the Persians reached Thermopylae, Sparta sent just 300 middle-aged men, under Leonidas, to defend the vital pass, promising that the rest would join them after the Games were over. Leonidas bravely tackled the Persian army on the vital road leading to southern Greece. In the epic two-day battle the slaughter was terrible. The Persians, hampered by their great numbers, trampled each other in their efforts to get at the 300 enemy. The Spartans fought with spears, swords, then with their fists and teeth. But the battle could only end one way, and the Spartans perished.

The battle was, of course, no more than an irritant to the invading Persians, who swept on. But the Spartans' heroism inspired the Greeks. Their navy engaged the Persian fleet and inflicted considerable losses. But Athens had to be evacuated as the Persians advanced, and the invaders set fire to the buildings on the Acropolis. The Greeks retreated to the Isthmus of Corinth, where their fleet was able to attack and destroy the Persian fleet. Unable to obtain supplies, Xerxes was forced to retreat into Thessaly, and this gave the Greeks a valuable breathing-space. The next year the Persians again attacked Plataea, but they found the Greeks prepared and suffered a severe defeat. This land victory was followed by a naval battle near Samos, which the Greeks also won. The Persians retreated, and for the next 30 years the warfare between the two countries became intermittent and of a guerrilla nature. It was not until 450 B.C. that both sides agreed not to attack one another.

Although Persian power had been broken, Athens had not benefited morally from the war. Instead of championing Greek freedom, Athens, with its powerful fleet, became the overlord of a country that once more centred itself on the Aegean. There was still a lack of unity between Athens and Sparta, the greatest land force. Power in Athens had passed to a warrior named Cimon, but his attempts to unite the city-states of Greece into a loose military union called the Delian League proved unpopular and he was accused of being pro-Spartan.

Cimon was succeeded by one of the greatest Athenian leaders, Pericles, who was very popular with the people and became virtual head of the Athenian state. His leadership brought to Athens a period of calm which enabled the city to rebuild its strength. He insisted that Athens should be the leader of the Delian League, and indeed the city's wealth and naval power was such that the city-states gradually became absorbed into the Athenian empire. At the same time democracy within the city was improved, with greater public participation. Sculpture and architecture flourished, and the bas-reliefs, now known as the Elgin marbles—which decorated the Parthenon and are now in the British Museum—were executed during this period. The drama of Sophocles and Euripides became popular, and schools of philosophy also developed, with Socrates being one of the best-known thinkers of the time. Socrates' most famous pupil was Plato; Plato in turn was to teach Aristotle; and Aristotle was to become tutor to a young Macedonian prince called Alexander who was to make his own dramatic mark on the world.

This magnificent era ended with the death of Pericles and the second Peloponnesian War between Athens and Sparta—a prolonged and intermittent struggle that did not end until the eventual defeat of the Athenians by Sparta in 405 B.C. Sparta, now the dominant state, ruled its new empire with a harsh hand, but during all this renewed inter-state rivalry the kingdom of Macedonia, in northern Greece, was watching and waiting its chance to exploit the situation.

In 338 B.C., King Philip of Macedonia attacked southern Greece and took control of the entire country. He attempted to restore peace and culture to the country, but in vain. He also turned his military attentions towards the old enemy Persia, but before he could launch his planned attack he was assassinated, and his 20-year-old son, Alexander, ascended the throne.

There was a rapid series of revolts against what Athenians were calling 'merely a crazy boy', but the rebels of Thebes and the north were quickly crushed and then, with a powerful army of 35,000 men, the man who was to be called Alexander the Great crossed the Hellespont, freed Troy, and met the Persian army at Granicus. Alexander's troops scattered the Persians, although Alexander himself narrowly escaped death. Alexander then resolved to break the Persians' sea power by marching round to Egypt and capturing every enemy port on the way. En route he stopped at the Temple of Gordiun, where a complicated knot was reputed to hold the key to a continent. Whoever could untie the knot would rule Asia, it was said. Alexander sliced the knot in half with one stroke of his sword.

An attempt by the Persian king, Darius III, to stop Alexander's advance was broken at Issus, and Darius wrote to Alexander offering him one-third of his empire. Alexander spurned the offer, replying: 'You must address me as Supreme Lord of all Asia. If you claim your kingdom, stand and fight for it.'

Tyre, Gaza, and the Egyptian capital of Memphis all fell to Alexander. And on the Nile delta Alexander founded his own port, Alexandria. The 25-year-old monarch marched on to Libya, then turned back into Mesopotamia to meet a new challenge from Darius who now had a heavily equipped army including 200 chariots and some war elephants from India. Brilliant leadership enabled Alexander to break this Persian force at Gaugamela. Victorious, Alexander marched on unopposed to Babylon, at that time the greatest city in the world, and then to the rich and legendary Persian capitals of Susa, Persepolis, and Ectabana. The gold which Alexander captured he ordered to be turned into coins, which he and his men quickly spent.

There seemed to be no end to Alexander's wanderings. Although he now had the throne of Persia in his grasp, he marched on to western India, and might well have continued to the borders of China if disturbances in Persia had not compelled him to return to Babylon. There Greece, Macedonia and Persia were formally united when Alexander married a Persian princess, Roxana. But, while at Babylon, Alexander became ill—probably with malaria—and he died in 323 B.C.

Had he lived, Alexander could have brought peace to the Middle East. In fact his only natural heir, the child Roxana was carrying, was to be assassinated very quickly, and Alexander's own deathbed wish was that his kingdom should go 'to the strongest'. As a result his empire was divided between three Macedonian generals. Ptolemy took Egypt, and at once declared his independence from the rest; Seleucus took the Asian territories, apart from the lands on the Indian border where there had already been a revolt; and Cassander became King of Greece and its European colonies. The divisions, rivalries, and conquests which followed were to last until Greece became part of the Roman Empire.

Ptolemy proved to be the strongest of Alexander's successors, and the centre of Hellenic culture moved to Alexandria. Ptolemy's empire grew to include Libya, Palestine and Cyprus, and the magnificent lighthouse which he had built at the entrance to Alexandria harbour became one of the ancient wonders of the world.

In 280 B.C., the divided Greek mainland was once again threatened by the barbaric hordes to the north. Gauls from the Danube region swept into Macedonia, and Alexander the Great's homeland crumpled under their attack. The city-states of central Greece banded together to meet the aggressors, and once again decided to make a stand at the vital pass of Thermopylae. But the Gallic king, Brennus, rounded the pass and plunged on towards the religious centre of Delphi. In previous times of national crisis the mysterious Delphic oracle had not always proved accurate, or perhaps it was just that the oracle's enigmatic prophecies were misunderstood. This time, the oracle seemed as vague as ever. 'Let the barbarians come,' commanded the voice which was said to speak for Apollo. 'The care for these things falls on me and the white maidens'.

The Gauls came on, although their numbers became fewer as contingents broke off to raid villages and towns along the way. Only a few thousand Greeks were available to meet the apparently unstoppable horde as it fell upon Delphi. After a day-long battle, Brennus and his army decided to spend the night in the deep gorge below the shrine. And then, in one of the most dramatic moments in the drama-filled history of Greece, the 'white maidens' arrived—a thickening storm of snowflakes which strong winds swept into heavy drifts. The Gauls awoke to a blizzard, and as they slipped and slithered their way back up towards the shrine the Greeks fell upon them. The Gauls were scattered and destroyed, and only one-third of the original attacking force got out of the country alive.

Meanwhile, Pyrrhus, a Greek general who was a cousin of Alexander the Great's, was in southern Italy attempting to defend the Greek enclaves there against the power of an emergent Rome. He found to his surprise that he was up against a huge force of well-drilled and heavily armoured men, and although he scored some early successes against the Romans, Pyrrhus found that the cost was too great—they were Pyrrhic victories. He returned to Greece where Sparta, which shared many of the Roman ideals, had already forged a link with Rome.

Fascinated by Greek culture, appalled by the country's internal decay, and feeling itself threatened by the half-hearted Greek attempts to play at power-politics in the Mediterranean vacuum, Rome finally decided to protect the Greeks both from outside aggressors and from themselves. A powerful army under Flamininus won two victories over the Greeks, and in 196 B.C. Flamininus officially announced that Rome was now 'the protector' of Greece. When there was a revolt against Roman rule 50 years later, Corinth was levelled by Roman troops as an example to the rest of the country. The Greeks were forced to accept the inevitable as the Roman Emperor Augustus imposed the 'Peace of Rome' all the way from Britain to Babylon.

It was at this time that Christ was born in Bethlehem, and it is worth recalling that as Greek was the common language of the eastern Mediterranean at this time, Jesus must have known and used Greek. But despite the faith that the Apostle Paul, a Hellenized Jew, was to bring to Asia Minor, Thessaly, Athens and finally Corinth (where he formed a Christian community), it took 300 years for Christianity to take firm root in the eastern Mediterranean. While Christians were still being martyred in Rome, Roman emperors like Hadrian were worshipping the pagan Greek gods.

The religious breakthrough came when the Emperor Constantine was converted to Christianity and granted Christians religious freedom. To this day Constantine, who died in A.D. 337, is known to Greeks as the founding father of the Orthodox world. Fittingly the city which Constantine had built seven years before his death on the site of old Byzantium, on the western shore of the Bosphorus dividing Europe and Asia, was to become a place to which Greeks would always look both with love and pride. He called it Constantinople.

Constantinople, founded by a Roman but essentially an eastern city, flourished throughout the dark ages of Europe, an oasis of culture. Missionaries and teachers ventured into the Balkans and Russia, taking with them both a new alphabet and a new religion. The Byzantines—as the people under Constantinople's sway were called—made mosaic pictures with bits of glass embedded in wet plaster, a classic art form of which good examples can still be found in Constantinople (now called Istanbul), Ravenna in Italy, and at Daphni near Athens. Byzantine artists also practised fresco painting, the art form that was to spark the Italian Renaissance. Religious feelings were also expressed in small painted wooden panels called *icons*, the Greek word for 'images', which can still be found in the eastern Mediterranean.

Although it was a peaceful city, interested mainly in literature, the arts, learning, architecture and religion, Constantinople could be roused to anger. When the Persians and the wild tribes of Eurasia captured Jerusalem and carried off the Christians' holiest relic, the True Cross, the Emperor Heraclius quickly gathered an army and set out to recover it. In a campaign similar to Alexander the Great's he stormed into Persia and recaptured the Cross in 628.

With the collapse of the Roman Empire, Byzantium had become a largely Greek-speaking entity centred on Greece and the eastern Mediterranean. The region in general, and Constantinople in particular, was the scene of a series of power-struggles and intrigues, and by the year 1000 Byzantium was surrounded by enemies, with the Bulgars to the north, the emergent Saracens to the east and south, and its trading rival Venice in the west. The Emperor Basil broke the Bulgar's power in a savage battle, and a successor, Alexius I, beat off another attack, this time by Norman invaders from the west.

Alexius welcomed the First Crusade against the Turks, but rather than being its saviour the Crusades were to be the death of Byzantium. In the year 1204 the Venetians diverted the Fourth Crusade, originally aimed at the Holy Land, and hurled it against Constantinople. The city's gigantic and supposedly impregnable walls were breached and the city was sacked. During three days of pillaging and looting, the work of 800 years was undone.

Broken, Byzantium was divided into feudal states that did not last. Amazingly, there was a resurgence of Byzantine power when Michael Palaeologus recaptured Constantinople in 1261, and Byzantine culture was briefly reborn. But the revived empire was already doomed, because the trade routes that had been the city's arteries were now blocked or dominated by other states. In 1453 the Ottoman Turk Mahomet II laid siege to Constantinople and aroused hardly a murmur of protest from the rest of the world. Although foreign ships and their crews volunteered to help defend the city, Sultan Mahomet's troops were armed with cannons which breached the city walls. Mahomet took the city and marched on to capture Athens in 1456. The island of Rhodes, stronghold of the Knights of the Order of St John of Jerusalem, held out longest, but that too fell in 1522.

Although they were not cruel masters, the Turks treated the Greeks as second-class citizens. Under Turkish rule large Christian families had to give one son to the Turks to be brought up as a janissary, a group that formed an elite corps of Turkish troops. But the prophet Mahomet had ordered that his followers should allow religious freedom to Jews and Christians, so the Greek religion did not die.

Greek culture was also kept alive, and fittingly enough Venice, which had played a major part in the downfall of Byzantium, helped by giving asylum to many Greek intellectuals and classicists who fled. Only when the Ottoman Turks overreached themselves did things begin to change, however. In 1664 the Austrians beat the Turks decisively in a battle at St Gotthard. Venice saw its chance and overran the Peloponnese and Attica, and it was during this campaign that the Parthenon in Athens was partially destroyed—a Venetian shell falling into the temple which the Turks were using as a gunpowder magazine.

In the Greek heartland, where the population had been declining steadily for centuries, Greek Christian brigands hiding out in the mountains were beginning to make their presence felt. The Turks were forced to stop recruiting Greek children for the janissary corps, and as the Turkish military position declined so the Greeks took greater control of the commercial and political life of their country. Although the Turks now treated their Greek subjects as near equals, however, they were not going to give up their empire without a fight. In the eighteenth century Turkish troops recaptured the Peloponnese, and even Russian intervention on behalf of the people with whom they had Orthodox religious ties was to no avail.

But the social order was changing; the French Revolution stirred the hearts of the oppressed Greek people, and although at the Congress of Vienna the leaders of the great European powers agreed to shore up the crumbling Ottoman empire, Greek independence was becoming inevitable. On 25 March 1821, Archbishop Germanos of Patras officially proclaimed Greek independence, and the date is still celebrated as Greece's National Day.

There was immediate communal bloodshed, the echoes of which still reverberate around the eastern Mediterranean to this day. With the Peloponnese and many of the islands in Greek hands, there was fighting between the Turks and Greek and Albanian 'rebels' in the mountains of north-western Greece. The western powers once more looked on with indifference as bitter guerrilla warfare was waged in the wilder parts of Greece and on the waters of the Adriatic and Aegean where superior Greek seamanship played havoc with Turkish communications. This was the time when men like Goethe, Schiller, and Victor Hugo spoke out boldly for the Greek cause and when Lord Byron dreamed aloud 'that Greece might still be free'. But Greece needed the support of arms, not words, and Turkish patience was exhausted. An Egyptian mercenary, Mahomet Ali Pasha, was despatched with powerful sea and land forces to settle the issue. He seized Crete, then landed an army of 10,000 men on the Peloponnese. Greek resistance was crushed, and only the west coast port of Missolonghi—now a quiet fishing-village—held out. Among the defence forces was the volunteer Byron, who died there of a fever. When the Turks finally broke through Missolonghi's defences, the townspeople blew themselves up rather than surrender, and at last— too late—Great Britain, France and Russia were moved to act. In 1827 a combined fleet sailed into Greek waters with the intention of forcing Mahomet's son, Ibrahim, to withdraw and to aid the creation of a Greek state. Ibrahim chose to fight at a place called Navarino Bay, but this time he had met his match. The allied fleet went into action on 27 October, sank 60 of Ibrahim's ships without loss to themselves, and the Greek revolution was over.

International power-politics led to a certain amount of argument over precisely of what the new Greek state should be comprised. The country's first leader, John Capodistrias, a former Russian foreign minister born on Corfu, settled the issue with some smart internal land grabbing which eventually led to the international recognition of a Greece made up of the Peloponnese, central Greece, and the Cyclades islands. Thessaly, Crete and the Dodecanese remained under Turkish rule, and Corfu was a British protectorate. Even then, the rebirth of Greece was a painful affair. Many peasants, heavily over-taxed, paid the new Greek government the ultimate insult of emigrating to Turkish lands; and Capodistrias was to die the victim of an assassin's bullet.

The European powers then chose a seventeen-year-old Bavarian prince, Otto, to rule Greece, and he arrived in the country in 1833 with his own 'police force' of 3,500 Bavarian troops. At least this force was able to crush the armed bands that had been roaming the country and imposing their own 'rule', and they also managed to evict the remnants of the Turkish forces from Athens and make it the Greek capital once again. Constitutional monarchy was established in 1843, but there was a brief hiatus when Greece followed its age-old habit of embarking upon some dangerous international power-politics which turned the British against Otto. Otto abdicated, and in 1863 a Danish prince, George, was crowned George I, King of the

Hellenes—a title that firmly established the Greek claim to Greek-speaking lands beyond their borders.

To mark the accession of George, and their approval, the British ceded Corfu and the other Ionian islands to Greece. George forced upon the country a more democratic constitution, introduced full male suffrage and the secret ballot, and broke up the great estates. But the country remained poverty-stricken, and Greeks continued to emigrate. What is more, the Great Powers were still worried about the direction in which Greece would lean. When Crete at last threw out the Turks the island was refused permission to unite with Greece, and feelings ran so high that there was almost a civil war. It fell to the politician Eleutherios Venizelos to dabble in the murky waters of international diplomacy in search of a solution. Through a succession of Balkan alliances, he was able to persuade the Great Powers to recognize both Crete and the island of Samos as Greek territory. Rhodes, by now, had passed into Italian hands.

In 1913, the long reign of King George ended in another assassination, and Crown Prince Constantine, former Commander-in-Chief of the Greek army, came to the throne. But Constantine was married to a sister of the German Kaiser Wilhelm, and he also had a great professional respect for Germany's military power. As the First World War loomed, Constantine decided to play safe and side with Germany; Venizelos, who disagreed, was dismissed.

The country was split. Venizelos set up a rival government in Thessalonika, and with Allied help strong pressure was put on King Constantine. He retreated to Switzerland, and Venizelos quickly threw Greece into the war on the side of the Allies. At the Versailles Peace Conference, Venizelos earned his reward: a Greek enclave at Smyrna, on Turkey's Aegean coast, which Venizelos hoped would be a refuge for Greeks in that area. The idea was to prove disastrous. As a result of a national plebiscite King Constantine returned to Greece and decided to make up for past failures by launching a full-scale attack upon Turkey from the base at Smyrna. The Greek army suffered a shattering defeat and lost 50,000 men, while the enraged Turks turned upon the Greeks living in Anatolia and slaughtered them. Smyrna was captured, sacked and burned. King Constantine abdicated, an army junta seized power in Athens, then Venizelos was asked to pick up the pieces.

Once again Venizelos showed his mastery of the art of diplomacy. At a remarkable meeting in Switzerland, Greeks and Turks agreed to settle their differences by an exchange of population. About 1,250,000 Greeks in Anatolia were to return to Greece; 400,000 Turks were to leave Greek territory for Turkey. Despite the human problems which this involved, the exchange worked well, and Venizelos returned triumphantly to the office of prime minister. Only another army coup was to displace him, and he died in exile in 1936.

The new leader of Greece was an army general called Ioannis Metaxas, a dictator who modelled himself on Mussolini. But he was a man of far greater mettle than the Italian fascist leader, and he carefully avoided aligning Greece with the other fascist powers. After the Italian seizure of Albania in 1940 he seemed unmoved, and even attended a party at the Italian legation in Athens. Early next day, 28 October, the Italian ambassador called unexpectedly at his home and Metaxas, wearing only a bathrobe, opened the door himself. The ambassador asked for formal permission for Italian troops to cross into Greece, a move which whould have linked Greece inextricably with Germany and Italy. Gently, General Metaxas shook his head. '*Ochi*' (no), he said, then shut the door in the ambassador's face. It was a moment Greeks still love to recall, and 28 October is now a national festival known as Ochi Day.

When the inevitable fighting began, the highly regarded Italian army proved no match for the Greek forces and was forced back into the Albanian mountains. Only the intervention of powerful German forces saved the Italians from a humiliating defeat, and in the spring of 1941 the Germans completed their occupation of Greece. The Greeks responded with savage guerrilla warfare, in which they had had long practice. The Germans responded by ordering the mass execution of civilian hostages. Fighting was particularly severe in remote spots like the mountains of Crete, where even to this day German tourists receive a cool welcome in many villages.

But as German power waned and defeat grew nearer, the Greek resistance fighters turned against each other. Half of them remained loyal to the Crown, but a strong Communist faction gained the upper hand and for a time at the end of the Second World War it looked as though Greece, now reunited with Rhodes and the Dodecanese islands, might be among the countries which were to disappear behind the Iron Curtain. British troops were forced to intervene to prevent the fall of Athens, and there was a massive influx of American arms and money. The Communist powers finally decided to abide by the Yalta Agreement, which placed Greece and Turkey firmly in the western sphere of influence, and Yugoslavia acted decisively by closing its border to the rebels. In 1949 the Civil War finally ended—but in terms of lives it had been more costly to Greece than the whole of the Second World War.

Today, Greek rivalries live on—partly as a result of recent history but partly, no doubt, because of long memories and fiery Greek temperament. In the north, and particularly in the big industrial cities of the mainland, the left is still predominant. But in the islands, as in Athens and in the villages of the mainland, the people are more interested in the virtues of peace and prosperity than in politics. In 5,000 years, this part of the world has seen too much strife.

History has left its mark. A Greek will quickly offer you his friendship, but it will be many years before he offers you his heart. Apparently logical and philosophical, the people still put pride before reason; passions run high, and anger is not far below the surface if a Greek feels that he, or his country, is being insulted.

True anger, however, bears no relation to the daily slanging-matches the visitor will see between drivers or between waiters and their customers. It often seems impossible to ask for directions, or even ask the time, in Greece without attracting a crowd of people who will offer conflicting advice, shout, and wave their arms about. Few Greeks will admit that they do not know the answer to a question, which may account for the conflicting advice.

However friendly they may appear to western visitors, the Greeks feel, with some justification, that history has misused them, and that when they try to justify their claim to the Hellenic world—which, of course, includes both the island of Cyprus and large chunks of Turkey—nobody understands them. Hellenism is an emotive subject to Greeks everywhere.

And yet despite apparently expansionist intentions, Greece is essentially a country of peace—a peace that is particularly apparent in the islands scattered over the glittering seas. They were a part of the stormy history described on the previous pages, and often the islanders were the principal sufferers. Now they are content to fish or farm a little, and sit for hours over their evening drinks arguing among themselves about past and future glories not on the battlefield but on the football field.

The Greeks are delighted to see visitors. They will not expect you to know their history or understand their problems, any more than they will expect you to know their language—although they will be pleased and flattered if you try.

Wise official counsels have, in recent years, added to these natural advantages when it comes to attracting tourists. Hotels are graded by the government and standards are fairly rigorous, especially in the state-owned and often cheap Xenia hotels. Roads may vary from the excellent to the appalling, but directional roadsigns either bear place-names in both the Greek and Roman alphabets or else are repeated in the Roman alphabet a few yards farther on, so you are unlikely to get lost except perhaps in the smallest, most outlying islands. Modern ferries mean that you can take either your own car, or an expensive hired car, almost anywhere in Greece. The ubiquitous *taverna* means that meals are never a problem.

The very existence of *tavernas* mean that self-catering holidays, in a rented flat or bungalow, are particularly attractive in Greece: you can breakfast in your holiday home, have a picnic lunch on the beach, and eat out almost every evening for little more than the cost of housekeeping at home. Islands which are particularly suited to this sort of holiday are mentioned individually later in this book, but the rapid growth in the availability of self-catering accommodation means that it is worth checking with a travel agent before you go. One tip: it is often very difficult to find self-catering accommodation once you actually arrive in Greece, and local impresarios push prices up to their limits if they find themselves in a sellers' market—especially in the high season; so book your flat or bungalow before you leave home. With advance booking you also get the benefit of inclusive flight, or other travel arrangements. Various British tour operators specialize in this kind of holiday: notably Owners' Services Ltd. (O.S.L.), and the Thomson Holidays 'Small and Friendly' programme.

The National Tourist Organization of Greece is also very helpful, and deals with individual inquiries. Its London offices are at 195 Regent Street, W.1 (Tel: 01–734 5997). In Greece, the tourist board is known as E.O.T., and it has offices on all the main holiday islands as well as its head office in Athens (2 Amerikis Street).

Besides the more usual ways of helping holidaymakers, E.O.T. is responsible for the tourist police. More countries should have tourist police—they are a marvellous innovation.

The task of the tourist police is, quite simply, to help tourists—and to enable them to fulfil this not-too-onerous task they have all the powers of an ordinary policeman. You will find tourist police offices at all main cities, ports and airports on the principal islands, as well as on the smaller islands during the holiday season. You can't find a room for the night? You've lost your purse? Your child is sick? Just ask a policeman—or, rather, a tourist policeman.

It might sound unnecessary, but in a country where you have to be wearing a uniform before anyone will take any notice of what you say, the tourist police are essential—perhaps due to some sort of rule about its taking an official to catch an official. *In extremis*, I have discovered, you can even persuade a tourist policeman to find a parking space for you, although I would imagine that they normally have more important things to do.

But as an example of just what magic the tourist police can work, they find beds in private houses for thousands of youngsters every year who arrive on the islands late at night with only a few hundred drachma.

And once, not so very long ago, I hitched a lift to Greece on a cruise ship, which I left at a minor Greek port. There the customs officials decided that not only were my movements suspicious, but so was the fact that I was carrying three cameras. After prolonged questioning they ordered that I should be searched and detained, pending inquiries. Angrily, I demanded that they should call the tourist police, and within a few minutes a policeman—an avuncular figure—arrived. I explained to him that I was a tourist, and asked if this was the sort of reception that tourists could expect in Greece.

That did the trick. The avuncular figure apologized without even listening to the customs officials, and told me that I could go. He then treated the officials to the most un-avuncular dressing-down that I have ever heard in Greece—or anywhere else for that matter. It was just the kind of support that one dreams of in the kind of situation that a holidaymaker fears most, and Greece is to be congratulated on being a jump ahead in the tourist field in that respect.

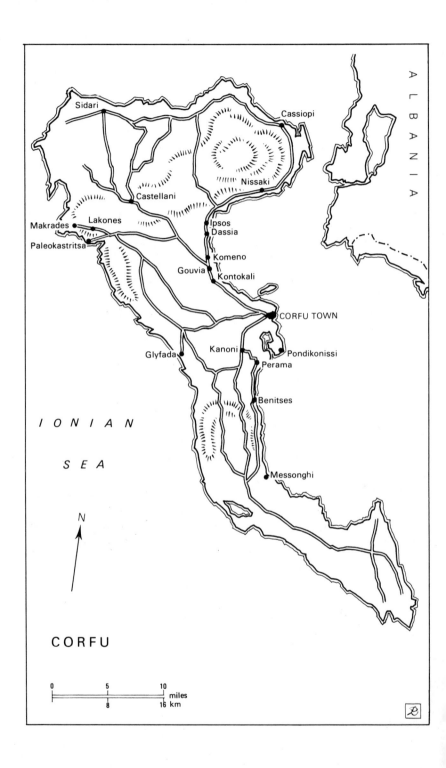

ALBANIA

Sidari

Cassiopi

Nissaki

Castellani

Makrades
Lakones
Ipsos
Dassia

Paleokastritsa

Komeno

Gouvia
Kontokali

CORFU TOWN

Kanoni
Pondikonissi
Perama

Glyfada

Benitses

I O N I A N

S E A

Messonghi

N

CORFU

0   5   10
                        miles
        8   16 km

2 CORFU

There was the solid *thwack* of willow smiting leather, and the red cricket-ball sped across the turf towards the boundary with a white-flannelled figure in vain pursuit. The crowd around the ground applauded politely. In the distance the strains of a brass band playing military music filtered through the hum of conversation.

A scene from rural England? A Victorian memory? No, this was Corfu, largest and most northerly of the Ionian islands off the northwest coast of Greece, on a typical Saturday afternoon in summer. For an accident of history has meant that Corfu—after Athens the most popular holiday destination in Greece for Britons—has a strangely British air about it.

A lush, green, and sometimes humid island, Corfu lies just off the Adriatic coast where Greece shares a common border with the forbidden country of Albania. Many of the tourists—half of them British—who arrive in Corfu in the charter planes that land at the airport every summer afternoon, or who make the ferry crossing from Italy or the mainland Greek port of Igoumenitsa, probably feel that they are visiting an island which is typically Greek. But Corfu can never be said to epitomize Greece.

Although the people are unquestionably Greek, Corfu has more in common with the other countries of the Adriatic than with mainland Greece, and the island's landscape, atmosphere and manners are western. No doubt this is largely due to Corfu's history, for over the centuries it has been conquered by the Goths, the Romans, the Normans, the Venetians, the Turks, the French, and finally by the British. The 50 years of British rule ended in 1864 when Corfu and the other Ionian islands were finally reunited with Greece, but Britain left behind a legacy in the shape of those three nineteenth-century staples: cricket, chutney and ginger beer.

Cricket is still played on the Esplanade Square in Corfu Town every summer Saturday afternoon, and attracts large and appreciative crowds of Corfiotes and visitors alike. Once upon a time, MCC

teams on their way by ship to India or Australia used to stop at Corfu
for a practice game or two, but today opposition is sparse and the
three local clubs—Byron, Gymnasticos, and a team called Feax after
the original inhabitants of Corfu—are delighted when they are chal-
lenged by visiting naval sides or by the scratch elevens made up every
year by organizations like British Airways. They also organize an
annual cricket festival in September, when British clubs take part
and some of the great names in the game compete. The last time I was
there the Corfiotes were awaiting with bated breath the impending
arrival of Fred Trueman—and I am only sorry that I could not stay
to see what the fiery fast bowler made of a pitch that, due to some
local dispute or other, had degenerated into a square of sun-baked
red earth interspersed with occasional patches of grass.

If the locals' resistance was braver than he expected, it may have
been due to the ministrations of Spyros (more than half of the men in
Corfu are called Spyros, for reasons that will soon become apparent), who dispenses pink-coloured courage behind the bar of what
Corfu's cricketers think of as 'their' hostelry: a cramped corner of
Tsirigotis's rather smart grocery store in town. There Spyros dispenses his own potent cocktail called *seconouzal*, which is made up of a
mixture of *Metaxa* brandy, bitter red Italian 'Chinamartin' and soda
water. Strictly speaking, Tsirigotis's is not a bar at all, but cricketers
will find a welcome and plenty of their own kind there.

Besides cricket, Corfu has another reminder of its colonial past.
The Esplanade resounds at weekends to the clamour of a brass band
playing on a garishly painted Victorian bandstand. And in the
nearby *tavernas* the favourite non-alcoholic drink is still ginger beer—
sweeter and more refreshing than its modern British counterpart,
and now known in idiomatic Greek as *tsintsi birra*.

Corfu even has a western European climate, for although the summers are sunny, dry and often stickily warm, the winter months can
be very wet and even the National Tourist Organization of Greece,
which is not quick to confess to bad weather, recommends that visitors to the island between November and February should pack a
mackintosh and an umbrella. The island benefits from its wet winters, however, by being blessed with a richly green landscape dominated by cypress trees and by myriads of olive trees which are said to
total three million. Corfiotes, anxious to impress, scoff at this meagre
total and insist: 'There are many more than three million olive trees
on our island.'

The only other thing that Corfu has in abundance is menfolk with the name of Spyros. They are named after Aghios (St) Spiridon, an import from Cyprus whose mortal remains were smuggled out of Istanbul in a sack and transferred to the glass-topped silver coffin that now reposes amid sputtering candles in the small, red-domed church of St Spiridon, the island's 'cathedral' in the old Venetian quarter of Corfu Town.

A number of miracles are ascribed to St Spiridon, including the breaking of the siege of Corfu in 1716 when a Greek and Italian force of 5,000 men and a violent storm combined to put paid to the Turkish fleet and an attacking army 30,000 strong. In a rather grisly ritual, the remains of St Spiridon are still paraded around the town four times a year, but after 400 years of such treatment the ageing saint is beginning to look badly in need of both a rest and, hopefully, a decent burial.

The Venetian parts of Corfu Town are the most attractive. Although the Venetian citadel, the Palaion Frourion, which dominates the eastern seafront is still a military establishment, it has been given the vestiges of beauty by allowing the moat or canal, which in fact turns the citadel into an island, to be used as a makeshift yacht marina. There is another fortress, the Neon Frourion or New Fortress, on a hillside dominating the harbour, with a fine view over the town and an early-morning market at its foot. To the north of the modern parts of the town one can also wander for hours through the narrow but attractive streets of the Venetian quarter, where bridges link the houses, ornate balconies catch the evening sun, washing hangs in profusion, and tiny vineyards flourish in the corners of walled gardens. You will get lost, but before long you will find yourself in the main shopping streets again.

One square in the old town hides the seventeenth-century Well of Kremasti, which bears the inscription in both Latin and modern English: 'This was made by Antonio Kokkini to help the people. 1699.'

It would be nice if the architectural bequests of British rule were as attractive. Alas, Corfu was governed largely by military gentlemen who were lacking in taste and somewhat over-endowed with a desire for self-glorification. The Royal Palace, or Palace of St Michael and St George, an ugly building that dominates the north side of the Esplanade, or Plateia, was built between 1819 and 1823 by Sir George Whitemore, the colonel of a British regiment stationed on the island, to serve as the treasury of the newly created Order of St Michael and St George and as a residence for the high commissioner. It later became a royal palace, and then the seat of the Ionian Senate. After the departure of the British, the Britannia emblem on the roof was pulled down, leaving the building with a peculiarly cock-eyed appearance, and it is a pity that although the state rooms were restored in the 1950s they cannot be visited at present. One wing contains a collection of Chinese and Japanese porcelain belonging to the Greek Ministry of Education, and some local mosaics can also be seen there. Otherwise the building is a white elephant going sorely to waste.

Dispirited Britons may at this point be reminded by loyal Corfiotes that the British brought to Corfu Town the benefits of paved roads, a hospital, a prison, piped water and piped sewage. But it is only fair to add that they also brought the appallingly ugly Ionian rotunda, near the bandstand, that was built by Sir Thomas Maitland, the erstwhile British high commissioner on the island, who was popularly known as King Tom because of his autocratic ways. Living up to his reputation, King Tom built the rotunda in memory of himself.

From an archway beside the Royal Palace a clifftop road curves dramatically around the northern tip of Corfu Town and dips down to the harbour, giving some picturesque views of the northern part of the island and across to Albania and the Greek mainland. Just beyond the Palace is one of the most elegant spots in the town: the superb Venetian building that houses the Rotary Club and the Corfu Reading Society. The latter was founded in 1846 and is the oldest intellectual society of its kind in Greece. It boasts a collection of 20,000 books on Ionian history and literature, and the fine arts, many of them in English. They are under the care of the Society's secretary, Mr Nondas Stamatopoulos, who speaks perfect English and welcomes serious students and enthusiasts to this unique library.

At the other end of the town, close to the superb Corfu Palace Hotel, is the island's museum, which is open on weekdays and on Saturday mornings throughout the year. This contains a wealth of finds from Garitsa cemetery and excavations at Mon Repos. The statuary, mostly Roman copies of Greek originals, is not particularly memorable, but the Hall of the Gorgon is worth seeing.

Besides the Swiss-run Corfu Palace Hotel, the island's best, Corfu

Town has a big range of hotels and restaurants. Most of the principal resort hotels are out of town, but in town try the Venetian-styled 'A'-grade Cavalieri, which is centrally situated, or the small 'C'-grade Hotel Calypso which is very clean, cheap, and close to the seafront.

For eating out, Corfu Town has both *tavernas* and more traditional western European-style restaurants. I like the Rex restaurant, and the Akton *taverna*/restaurant on the quay which has an interestingly international menu but which, last time I was there, was mysteriously unable to produce that most universal of all Greek beverages, Greek coffee. Local dishes include *pastitsaada*, meat served with macaroni in a special tomato sauce, and *sofrito*, veal stewed in a thick white sauce with parsley and garlic.

I also like the Aigli restaurant, which has the advantage of being situated in one of the most attractive spots in Corfu Town, the arcaded west side of the main square which includes the cricket ground. This dates from the French occupation of the island and is a blatant copy of the Parisian colonnades. Souvenir-shops and cafés peep out from under the colonnades, and turning this side of the square into a traffic-free zone has put it firmly on the route of the island's *volta*.

The *volta*, or evening stroll, takes place all over Greece, and in many of the smaller islands it is an important social occasion, especially on Sundays. Traditionally, families dress up in their best clothes and take an evening walk along the main street, getting a breath of fresh air at the end of the day and meeting and greeting friends and acquaintances. Once the *volta* was a sort of marriage market too, with over-protected girls having perhaps their only chance of the day to nod or smile at eligible young men. In cosmopolitan Corfu, this charming habit could well have died a natural death. Instead, the Corfiotes have adapted it to the 1980s: as the swifts wheel and scream over the rooftops, islanders and holidaymakers alike stroll around the Esplanade, laughing and joking after a day in the sun. You can stop for a cool beer or an *ouzo* outside a café, talk to friends, make new acquaintances and plan for tomorrow. You may not even realize that you are part of the *volta*—and that is just as it should be for it is a totally spontaneous event.

Less spontaneous is another of the traditional sights of Corfu Town: the horse-drawn *monippo* (literally: one horse) carriages, the horses bedecked in brightly coloured straw hats through which their long dark ears poke absurdly and which somehow contrive to make them look like ageing tarts. The *monippos* tout for business in the town centre and around the docks, and their drivers have the advantage of being able to find their way around the back-streets. But riding in a *monippo* can be an expensive business, and photographing them can be expensive too, for the driver will pursue you with demands for money if he should catch you snapping his horse.

Because bus services are erratic at the best of times, and virtually non-existent on Sundays, you need some sort of vehicle in which to get around Corfu. Car hire is expensive, and may be even more expensive if you try to park in town—the one occasion on which you are likely to find a policeman. Unusually for Greece, the police are remarkably unobtrusive in Corfu Town; it is one of the few towns with a municipal police force and therefore able to determine its own policies. In Corfu, the police prefer to keep a low profile—except when dealing with parking offenders. That is as it should be on an island where crime is virtually unknown. Theft and vandalism are very rare on Corfu, and in country areas there is no need to lock up your car or the doors and windows of a rented house or flat. The Corfiotes say, with some justification, that if there is any trouble it is almost invariably caused by visitors to the island. The authorities try to keep trouble-makers out of Corfu but, just in case, the small off-shore island of Vido is used as a prison. There are, as everywhere in Greece, special tourist police to help and advise visitors.

Car hire prices have helped to bring about a mini-boom in the hire of bicycles and mopeds, the latter of which cost about one-fifth of the price of a hired car and can be seen puttering their way all over Corfu. On a hilly island 40 miles long and up to 20 miles wide, the moped has many advantages. But with steep, stony tracks leading down to many beaches, accidents are fairly common among people who are unused to being on two wheels, and both moped-riders and cyclists often bear the scars of their travels on their knees or elbows. The Corfiotes, now well used to the sound of mopeds toppling on to gravel, can be relied upon to offer instant sympathy and medicaments. But while your arm is being dabbed with a soothing lotion it is worth checking up on what exactly the lotion is. A friend who took a tumble in a tiny village was tended by an ancient crone who muttered unintelligible words of comfort while pouring a sticky brown liquid on to the assortment of cuts and grazes. Smiling toothlessly, the crone then pointed proudly to the label on the bottle, which read:

'Expectorant linctus.' The cuts and grazes, one should add, mended with surprising speed.

All roads lead to Corfu Town but, that advantage excepted, the island's road system leaves much to be desired. That again is the fault of the British. The military built roads all right, but they built them for their own convenience rather than the islanders'. As a result, the best roads lead principally to the beauty-spots and picnic areas that were frequented by the military and civil administration. But the east-coast roads are good, as are those to the airport.

South of Corfu Town the road passes through the peaceful landscape of Kanoni; skirts the lagoon of Halikiopoulou which is separated from the sea by a long narrow causeway; goes past a shorter breakwater which leads to the white convent on a tiny islet; overlooks the cypress-girded chapel on Pondikonisi, or Mouse Island—the subject of tens of thousands of Corfu holiday postcard pictures and holidaymakers' photographs—and skirts the international airport. Mouse Island is more attractive from the shore than it is to the visitor making the short boat-crossing to it; but it is one of two claimants to a starring role in the story of Odysseus, for legend says that it is Odysseus's ship turned to stone.

The airport is bursting at the seams, and its approach and situation also make it unpopular with pilots. As well as its proximity to Albanian airspace, it has a hair-raising approach over the sea—one of a number of such airports in Greece. Corfu is presently planning a new airport, which seems certain to be built on the southernmost tip of the island. This no doubt will ease the problems for pilots, and one hopes that it will also bring to an end the non-stop scramble in the luggage hall which is many visitors' introduction to Greek manners and Greek inefficiency. But unless there is a dramatic improvement in Corfu's roads, which seems unlikely, it will also mean an hour's drive to Corfu Town and a two-hour drive for anyone staying in the far north of the island—a most unwelcome innovation.

Close by are the overrated Hilton Hotel and the beautiful royal villa of Mon Repos. Situated in a park overlooking the sea, Mon Repos is another legacy of the British occupation of Corfu: it was built for Sir Frederic Adam in 1824, became the summer residence of the British high commissioners, and later passed into use as a summer holiday-home for the Greek royal family. Prince Philip was born in the villa in 1921. You cannot go inside, but it is still worth looking at, and it has the advantage that just below it is a well-equipped public beach—the best within easy reach of town.

About twelve miles south of Corfu Town is the extraordinarily ugly Palace of Achilleon, built on a wooded promontory overlooking the sea in 1890 for Empress Elisabeth of Austria, and bought by the German Kaiser Wilhelm II in 1907. Its interior, kept as a museum, is a monument to bad taste, complete with such oddities as a throne-like lavatory and a desk with a riding-saddle as its chair. Outside the main entrance to the palace is a huge marble statue called Achilles Wounded, on the pedestal of which the Kaiser had engraved the modest inscription: 'To the greatest of Greeks from the greatest of Germans' (an inscription later removed). Today the palace also houses a casino, which you need your passport to enter.

From the attractive wooded grounds it is only a short walk down to the fishing-village of Benitses, situated among olive groves and now a popular centre for self-catering villa holidays. Besides its setting, Benitses undoubtedly owes much of its popularity to its friendly population, who will quickly make you feel at home in their excellent *tavernas* which specialize in fish dishes. Benitses has a good beach, as does the ancient village of Messonghi further south.

Beyond Messonghi, Corfu becomes narrow, predominantly flat, and uninteresting, although there are some good beaches to be found if you are willing to explore. A better excursion, however, would be across the waist of the island to the ancient village of Pelekas built high above the coast so that the villagers would have ample warning of attacks by the pirates who once infested Greek waters. Above the village is a parking-space and steps leading up to a lookout built for the Kaiser, who liked to go there in the evening to enjoy the view and the sunsets.

There are more fine views from the promontory of Paleokastritsa (literally: old castle) on the west coast of the island with its small, pebbly bays and smart hotels and restaurants. On a headland to the north there is a picturesque monastery. The best views of Paleokastritsa itself are from the village of Lakones, at the top of a steep winding road.

Although all the roads are signposted, usually in Greek and English, this side of the island is a maze of wooded hillsides and steep bays which are fun to explore but in which it is all too easy to get lost. But find your way if you can to the Grand Hotel Glyfada, which dominates the western side of the island and has a huge sandy beach, a real afternoon suntrap. The hotel itself is run by the Bouas family, who have taken the bold step of lavishly furnishing it with family antiques; if it were not for the transport problems, which effectively trap you there, particularly on Sundays, this would have to be my favourite hotel on Corfu.

The northern part of the island is dominated by the 3,000-feet-high peak of Pantokrator, from the summit of which it is possible to see both the Italian coast to the west and the mountains of Macedonia in the east. A footpath from Nissaki leads up the mountain, and is a fairly easy walk.

Pantokrator effectively cuts the north of the island in two. You can follow the coast road up through Kontokali (where the Kontokali Palace Hotel is another of my personal favourites), to Dassia (two fine Chandris hotels), Ipsos (a Club Méditerranée where topless antics have failed to stir the Corfiotes despite the fact that they are illegal) and Nissaki to the pretty fishing-village of Cassiopi. Or you can go inland, climbing up to Korakiani before dropping down to the north-western coastal villages.

The coast road, particularly in the far north, is an interesting and attractive drive, twisting through valleys and soaring precipitously round sheer rock-faces in its own minor challenge to France's Corniche and Italy's Amalfi drives. Only three miles across the water—so close that at times you feel you could throw a stone down on to it—lies Albania.

Some of the hotels that have sprung up along this route, particularly those closest to Corfu Town, are not to be recommended. It is wise, too, to look twice at any self-catering accommodation that might tempt you, and particularly at its situation. At Ipsos, for example, there is some really excellent accommodation, but the village itself has become untypically garish and noisy, with some very poor *tavernas*, and although it is on a big sheltered bay there is only a narrow shingle beach.

Because of its hotels and its accessibility, this stretch of coast has become the centre of Corfu's night-life. But it is a night-life of extremes. You can dine superbly at the Restaurant Bistro on the northern edge of Corfu Town and close to the harbour, where restauranteur George Apostoleris has set a very high standard, but a mile or two up the road you might wait for up to three hours even to get served in one of the catch-penny *tavernas* that offer Greek dancing. This dancing, incidentally, is a feature of *tavernas* and not of restaurants, and pre-planned displays of it are something which many find disappointing. Although on Corfu you can see impromptu displays of *sirtaki*, the soulful Greek dance which men traditionally perform on their own, it is at its best in the smaller islands or in Crete. If you do see the real thing, the two golden rules are not to join in (unless you are Greek and know what you are doing) and not to applaud; but in Corfu they will forgive either—and may even encourage them.

Scattered along the coast road the night-clubs, such as they are, are usually ramshackle-looking buildings with extremely loud disco-type music interspersed by 'ethnic' floorshows. They are not too expensive, and relatively harmless, but I cannot say that I have ever enjoyed visiting one. The best, if you are determined to be a swinger, is Corfu By Night.

But perhaps one of the most attractive things about Corfu is that it does somehow manage to cater for all tastes. On this same stretch of road, dotted with unattractive—and even un-Greek—*tavernas*, I have found at least two havens and I am sure that there are many more. One is at Dassia where, for reasons best known to themselves, a young couple have built a *taverna* in the middle of a field and reached only by a stony path. I picked my way carefully along this path one summer's evening for a much-needed pre-dinner beer, and stayed on to watch the sunset—and miss dinner because the owners insisted upon serving the beer with a traditional *mezethes*, or snack, of black olives, *feta* cheese, and long thin slices of cucumber. Be warned: such indulgence can lead to a glass of *ouzo*, a long and multilingual conversation with the *taverna* owner or one's neighbours at the next table, another *ouzo*. . . .

My other haven is at Ipsos, where I once stayed in a borrowed flat on my own while doing some work. There was a small *taverna* next door, which stayed open only during the day and was used principally as a lunch-time bar by the locals. The owner had heard, on the village grapevine no doubt, that I was alone, and was immediately concerned. He cornered me and issued his instructions: 'For breakfast you will come to me. At nine every day. I will be waiting.' As good as his word there were fruit juice, hot croissants and French coffee awaiting me at nine the next morning and every morning thereafter. I paid him, of course—but he would accept only a token payment, and that only after much argument. In a less cosmopolitan island than Corfu he might well have refused payment altogether and taken any insistence as an insult. In those circumstances, give a present (money will do) to the inevitable child or grandchild—it will delight your host.

There are problems of a different kind in the very un-Greek Pig and Whistle, a strange building on the northern edge of Ipsos which manages to look like a disused shack but which, in fact, contains a restaurant and bar. There, the large and fiercely moustached proprietor, Andreas, an individualist if ever there was one, serves you if he likes the look of you and ignores you if he does not. Andreas is popular with visiting Britons because of the colourful collection of British tea-towels, depicting every conceivable scene from Trooping the Colour to a Scottish croft, which festoon the ceiling of his bar. Despite having three or four helpers, Andreas likes to make out all the restaurant bills, serve all the drinks, and collect all the money himself, so service can be slow. But the Pig and Whistle is a cheerful, friendly place in which to spend an evening, and on an island where there is no official closing time it does have the advantage that you are left in no doubt about the time at which your evening's festivities end. Andreas calls 'time' by ringing a bell, blowing a whistle, and shouting 'Goodbye'. Hints don't come any bigger than that.

Perhaps one might think of the Pig and Whistle as the last outpost of 'touristy' Corfu, for things get a lot quieter north of Ipsos. One nice spot at which to stay might be Nissaki, which consists basically of three good *tavernas* and a small, but sometimes crowded, beach. There you can hire a *caique*, complete with skipper and not very expensive, to sail the last few leisurely miles to Cassiopi—a pretty spot that is being made even more attractive by some imaginative landscaping around the harbour but which, perhaps because the road goes no farther, tends to get rather busy.

There is a good quayside *taverna*, crowded at lunchtime, and several smaller establishments. The latter are the base for a number of *taverna* holidays now offered by several firms—and for the experienced traveller these are worth considering. The rooms, usually over the *taverna* in question, are clean, and it goes without saying that the meals are good. In Cassiopi, however, avoid the unattractive backstreets and remember that there are likely to be late-night revellers about even on the nights when you do not feel like revelling.

One advantage of sailing between Nissaki and Cassiopi is that many of the tiny beaches along this stretch of coastline are accessible from the land only with difficulty. With a boat you can stop and swim where you wish. There is no need to plan meals, for even where the 'village' is only a cluster of half-a-dozen houses, or even fewer, there is invariably a *taverna*—and the food, however basic, is inevitably good.

Inland, the hilly country around Korakiani is a delight. Not many holidaymakers seem to find their way there, perhaps because the roads are often unsuitable for moped riders. But if you don't have a car, get off your moped and walk. Or try a holiday which is actually based in this country area: it will have to be self-catering, of course, for there are no hotels, but in the inland villages 'self-catering' usually means an early morning stroll down the road to buy freshly baked bread and local honey for breakfast, planning a similar picnic lunch, and dining out in a *taverna* because that is as cheap as anything you could concoct for yourself.

There are beaches in this corner of Corfu—unspoilt, uncrowded coves that suffer only from the disadvantage of being stony rather than sandy. If you become a little footsore, there are alternative sandy stretches such as the one at the extreme western end of Aghios Georghios. A *taverna* at the eastern end of the beach attracts the visitors, and from the *taverna* it looks as though the beach makes a gradual transition from sand to stone, so few venture to the opposite end. In fact, the view is an illusion. There are stony patches, but they are interspersed by big empty stretches of sand. And, hidden from the eye, a sandy shelf extends gently from the water's edge for some way out to sea at thigh level.

Despite all the *tavernas*, Corfu is unlikely to be remembered for its gastronomic delights. With the exception of the island's leading restaurants, the food is simple—and even monotonous. Kebab or seafood, with the inevitable Greek salad made up of peppers, tomatoes, olives, and *feta* cheese. *Feta* is possibly an acquired taste, although it is one to which cheese-lovers will quickly adapt. It is a goats' cheese, with the texture of a good, crumbly Caerphilly, but wetter and with a distinctly salty flavour. You can buy it in most grocer's shops, where it is often spooned out of containers in ice-cream cabinets or something similar. Besides the specialities mentioned earlier, look out also for charcoal-grilled bass.

Besides the tourist police, visitors can seek advice from the local offices of E.O.T., the Greek tourism organization, which is at Diikitirion, in Corfu Town. Not all E.O.T. offices are as helpful or as informative as they might be, but the one on Corfu is very well run and the staff go out of their way to deal satisfactorily with questions and problems both large and small.

Its deputy director, Mr John Tranakas, offered this explanation for the island's popularity with British visitors: 'Not only is our history linked with that of Britain, but there is a large British community here,' he said. 'So it is, in a way, a little bit of home.'

He did not add that it is 'a little bit of home' with hot sunshine and a casual and relaxed air—an ideal introduction to Greece without being too Greek. What he did add, in a heart-catching farewell, was the same message which implicitly goes to all British holidaymakers: 'I hope you will come back to Corfu soon, to sit in the sun, and drink ginger beer—and perhaps watch the cricket.'

3 THE OTHER IONIAN ISLANDS

The harbourmaster was cross. He distinctly remembered telling the residents of Paxos that they could dump the residue from their olive presses into the island's beautiful, sheltered harbour only until the end of March. And here it was, May, and the water still had a suspiciously black, oily look.

He descended upon the island from neighbouring Corfu with a scowl as black as the water. Justice, he told me sternly as the ferry trundled across the few miles of the Adriatic that separates the two islands, had to be done.

Justice was indeed done. I got off the ferry at Lakka, a tiny, picturesque port on the northern tip of Paxos, which consists of Stefan Aperigis's harbourside *taverna*, a few houses and little else. By the time I had sipped a refreshing *ouzo*, looked round a bit and persuaded a taxi to take me the short distance across the island to the main port of Gaios, the residents of Gaios were smarting under the indignity of a few on-the-spot fines and a dressing-down from the harbourmaster. The atmosphere in the town was sullen.

Sitting alone outside a *taverna*, the harbourmaster looked sad. Why was he unpopular, he asked me. He was only doing his job. Then he had an idea.

'A party,' he exclaimed. 'We will have a party. Tonight, everybody is my guest for dinner.'

Which is how the harbourmaster and I, and what seemed like the entire population of Gaios, came to be eating fresh fish and drinking rough red local wine at the Rex Restaurant all evening and long into the night. Several holidaymakers joined the throng and were made welcome. The atmosphere became relaxed, then jolly, then distinctly hearty. The harbourmaster was a good host, there was no doubt about that.

Next morning, when I staggered back down to the harbour for a breakfast of fruit juice, sweet *loukoumas* doughnuts smothered in honey, and thick black coffee, the harbourmaster had gone on the morning ferry. The water in the harbour was a shade blacker than usual, due to the addition of the morning's residue from the olive presses. And the locals greeted me with warm smiles. 'The harbour-master,' said one, nodding wisely, 'is a good man.'

This pantomime, in which justice and honour were at stake far more than any real concern about the olive presses (the residue may stain the water, but it has none of other unpleasant side-effects of our own oil pollution) was, I discovered, symptomatic of the Ionian islands. At first glance the people of these north-westerly islands are blonder, more western European, more sophisticated than in the rest of Greece. But they are Greeks just the same—with the fierce pride of Greeks everywhere.

That, however, does not detract from the charm of Paxos or any of its Ionian neighbours. They are so near to the bustle of Corfu, yet they have remained almost untouched by tourism and (unless you count a few olive husks) they are the unpolluted, unspoilt, unchanging Greece that one expects of the Greek islands.

Paxos is an idyllic spot. Not much more than a sea-girt olive grove eight miles long and six wide, it houses a few visitors in what is often very basic self-catering accommodation in Lakka and in and around Gaios. For a slightly more civilized stay there is the Paxos Beach Hotel, hiding shyly among the trees on the water's edge a mile or so out of town.

A boat-trip round the island is a revelation. You start from Gaios harbour, protected from the sea by the rocky bulk of Aghios Nikolaos island which is separated from Paxos only by a long narrow chan-nel—giving the harbour the appearance of being on a river rather than the sea. Aghios Nikolaos is covered with golden broom in the spring, spreading an aphrodisiacal perfume over the entire town. At the water's edge yachts jostle for moorings with a handful of fishing-boats, for these are popular waters for sailing holidays to Greece.

Beyond Gaios are dozens of deserted beaches between the rocks, the olive groves, and the lines of tall cypresses marching down to the shore. In the Bay of Ozia the sea bubbles mysteriously—and health-ily, for there are underwater springs there that give bathers an unex-pected bonus.

Antipaxos is even lovelier—a tiny, two-mile-long island of olive trees, beaches, and some caves big enough for a small ship to sail into. There is some self-catering accommodation to let there, but the island is best visited as an excursion from Paxos.

Back in Gaios, I decided that the handful of British expatriates who make their home there for all or part of the year know what they are doing. For a truly relaxing holiday, it would be hard to think of a more ideal spot; nothing much happens on Paxos.

The locals have banded together to save the sixteenth-century church in the town square from collapsing, and in so doing have retained the charm of the harbourside square complete with its *tavernas* (the one closest to the water's edge is marginally the best) and its smattering of shops. The shops tend to operate on the principle of supply and demand rather than having any clearly identifiable role—if you want to change travellers' cheques, for example, the man to talk to is the proprietor of the hardware shop because he doubles up as island banker if he is not too busy.

Visitors are limited to eating, sleeping, swimming, playing *tavli* (backgammon, Greek-style), watching the evening performance put on among the olive trees by the flickering firebugs, listening to the asthmatic braying of donkeys, and picking their way home through the maze of netting which is put up to ensure that none of the olive crop goes to waste.

Besides the varied selection of *caiques* and small car ferries serving Corfu, Paxos is linked with the other Ionian islands and the mainland port of Patras by a big, fast car ferry, the *Ionis*, which calls there twice a week. The *Ionis* is too large to nose her way into Gaios harbour, and instead uses a new jetty half a mile out of town. The advantages of travelling light in the Greek islands soon become apparent as you pick your way along the stony track leading to this landing-stage, but one's own discomfort vanishes as one watches the seamanship required to back an ocean-going ship up against a stone dock lit by one solitary calor-gas lamp and the headlights of a couple of cars. The manoeuvre reminds one that it is best to allow some elasticity in one's travelling plans in this part of the world—for the *Ionis* will not stop at Paxos in anything but the calmest of weather.

Travelling south through the Ionian islands, the mood and the scenery change. After Antipaxos comes Lefkas, which just qualifies as an island because it is separated from the Greek mainland only by a marshy isthmus and a canal. But it does have the individuality of an island, and the annual festival of art and literature in August has proved a big attraction. Lefkas is reached by a chain ferry linking causeways on the island and on the mainland. One's first impression is a feeling of disappointment, for it is not as beautiful a spot as guidebooks and pamphlets suggest. Earthquake damage in 1948 is largely to blame, for many of the island's man-made beauties were destroyed then, including a lot of property in the Turkish-style town of Lefkas. Unfortunately, the local residents have not helped matters by making repairs to their close-packed timber-framed houses with chunks of corrugated iron, and the open drains can only add to the visitor's distaste.

Fortunately, the works forged by a mightier hand than man's are still attractive, and the glorious 13-mile coastal drive to the Bay of Vliko confirms this. En route, at Nidrion, there are rooms to let in the houses above the steeply shelving pebble beach, and a good grill-house. There is also a fine view of the small islands scattered between Lefkas and Ithaca, which include the well-guarded private family island of Skorpios, where shipping magnate Aristotle Onassis married Mrs Jackie Kennedy is 1968 and was buried in 1975. The island is so secret that it does not even appear on some local maps, but the fishermen of Lefkas, cashing in on curiosity, will take visitors around the 'Onassis island' fairly cheaply.

Beyond Vliko the roads are badly signposted, and it is hard to find one's way. The tenacious will reach the vast, empty, sandy beaches around places like Sivota, where a little restaurant specializes in fresh lobster, and Vassiliki, where the price of a bed for the night in a private house bedecked with a flower-filled balcony is so cheap as to be laughable. A romantic spot, in the true sense of the word, is the Leap of Lefkas, where the paths of criminals and lovers once crossed. The criminals had to leap into the sea from the clifftop to prove their innocence; the lovers traditionally made the leap to cure unrequited love and, as the poetess Sappho is said to have discovered, the cure was often permanent—for the cliff is 236 feet high.

Mountainous Ithaca is, of course, the island of Odysseus. But Homer, author of the *Odyssey*, did not seem to see it as a tourist spot. He described it as 'a precipitous isle, unfit for horses . . . poor for goats . . .'. I hesitate to contradict the epic poet, but I found it utterly charming.

It won't ever be a major holiday destination, but the lucky few will find it and fall in love with it and with its simple charm. But then, who could fail to fall in love with an island where a ship's captain, mocked by his friends on shore for docking awkwardly in a high wind, responds by spinning his vessel round in its own length in the harbour to save 'face' (to appreciative applause from the onlookers)?

Or where, on the deserted Skinos beach, a local smallholder brings one an unasked-for cup of afternoon coffee? Or where a *taverna* owner, having missed you one evening, asks anxiously next night: 'What happened to you? Was anything wrong with the last meal you had here?'

Or, above all, where they take such pride in the number 17 bus? I wanted to cross the island from the principal port of Vathi, and was given grave and prolonged instructions on how to go about the journey. 'Catch the bus in the town square,' the locals advised. 'The number 17. You will see the number on the front.'

I duly found the number 17 bus but, still unsure, asked the driver if it were the right one. He looked puzzled. 'We only have one bus,' he said, haltingly.

Then why did it carry the number 17? He looked even more puzzled, then said: 'But all buses have numbers, don't they?'

Perhaps he was not a landlubber, a rare breed on an island rich in naval traditions. Because Ithaca is unsuitable for farming, or indeed for anything much, its sons have taken to the sea and ranged the world. For this reason, if no other, visitors are made particularly welcome on Ithaca, and you cannot sit for long outside a *taverna* with a drink in your hand before one of the islanders stops to ask you where you are from and to say that he has been there himself, or knows someone who has. It is also a curiously relaxed island, full of little vignettes that serve to remind you that the Ionian islander sees no reason for rushing around.

This, coupled with the relative absence of any motorized traffic other than the three-wheeled carts so beloved of Greeks, is no doubt why one cyclist I saw felt perfectly safe to ride down the main street of Vathi drinking a cup of coffee—no mean feat of balance, when one comes to think about it. Besides Vathi—also known as Ithaca, just to help with the confusion—it is worth visiting some of the island's archaeological sites, as well as some of the spots identified, sometimes on rather dubious grounds, as the settings for various scenes from the Homeric legends.

Transport is scarce, and taxis are very expensive, so it is best to walk or cycle when possible. Skinos beach is a half-hour's brisk walk from the town, but worth the effort for it is picturesquely situated. Alternatively, local boatmen may ferry you to a picnic or swimming vantage-spot fairly cheaply.

Vathi itself is built, or perhaps scattered would be a better word, around its big, deep-water harbour and an island chapel. There are a couple of medium-size hotels, one of them named, predictably enough, the Odysseus, but rooms are so easy to come by, so clean and so cheap that it really is worth taking a chance. There are plenty of restaurants and *tavernas* in the town, and even a pizza parlour to remind one of the proximity of Italy. But supplies, even of essentials, can be erratic—a truism on all the Ionian islands except Corfu.

A natural channel, in places not much more than a mile wide, separates Ithaca from Kefalinia which is, in fact, the largest of the Ionian islands and can rival even Corfu for the variety and beauty of its scenery.

Car and passenger ferry services from Patras, Ithaca and Corfu use the little port of Sami, on Kefalinia's east coast nestling beneath a Venetian castle. Indeed, these ferries and the business they bring have created an air of prosperity about Sami, which has no other apparent reason for its existence. But beware, for accommodation and even eating facilities in the town itself are sparse.

A delay at Sami, however, can be put to good use, for two of the island's most remarkable attractions are close by. The first, less than two miles out of town and close to a couple of big resort-style hotels, is the Melissani Cave, which contains a dramatic and beautiful underground lake of crystal-clear azure water lit only by the sunlight glancing down from a hole in the roof 150 feet above. A surly youth was the cave's only custodian when I visited it, but once past him one descends to the lake by way of a sloping man-made tunnel which itself affords an attractive view of the lake. On the lake a rowing-boat, its oars muffled, waits to carry you into the inner cavern, where stalactites hover threateningly over the wreckage of an earlier boat that appears to have come to grief on an 'island' created by a massive rockfall. Despite its beauty, the Melissani Cave somehow has a chill and gloomy air about it, and crossing the Styx must have been rather like rowing into that underground cavern—except that I doubt whether Charon had to push his oars through an accumulation of cigarette-ends left in the water by earlier visitors.

I preferred the area's second great cave, the Cave of Drogarati, just over two miles from Sami. Large and imaginatively lit, this cave is known colloquially as 'the grave', and after a few moments walking between the stalactites and stalagmites one begins to understand why. An owl gazes mutely at you, and it is a second or two before you realize that it is a trick of the light reflected off a twisted stalactite.

You see another figure, a mother holding her baby, then a whole host of figures. They seem to be asleep, but as you pass more and more of them you feel that they have the stillness not of sleep but of death, like the carved figures on cathedral tombs. Finally, you come to the 'ramparts' of a fairytale castle—just another form into which the stalactites and stalagmites have convoluted themselves. There is an air of unreality about it all, and it comes as a relief to escape up the steps and out into the fresh air and sunshine again.

Infrequent buses and expensive taxis link Sami with Kefalinia's main port and capital, Argostoli, on the western side of the island across the Agrapidiaes Pass. Argostoli is a surprisingly modern town, having been rebuilt after suffering almost total destruction in an earthquake in 1953. It lies on one side of the long, deep, fjord-like Livadi Bay that splits the island into two uneven parts, and as the shallow Lagoon of Koutavos also laps the shores of the town, Argostoli is on a north-facing peninsula—a Greek oddity that makes it hard to get one's bearings at first . A 700-yard-long causeway and bridge across the lagoon provide a dramatic entry to the town, as well as cutting three miles off the old road journey.

Perhaps because it has so much sea frontage, the town clusters itself around an olive-fringed square with a massive palm tree at each corner and flamboyant statues of the politicians Metaxa and Volyannos. Here the island's schoolchildren, smartly uniformed like all Greek children, parade on big occasions to the music of a disjointed brass band playing, among other things, the familiar strains of *Roll out the Barrel*. You may also see the colourful Ionian costume being worn there for parades or dancing displays—a special treat on an island that is so brashly modern in many other respects.

There are several good hotels, especially the Xenia, in this central part of town, but I recommend the ungraded but comfortable Aenos Hotel. Its lack of classification is doubtless due to the fact that it does not serve meals of any kind, but these are easily obtained almost next door at the excellent Kefalos Restaurant, which also has plentiful supplies of the refreshing dry white Kefalinian wine, *Robola Cephalonie*.

The island's best hotel, the Mediterrane, is at Lassi, on the tip of the Argostoli peninsula and only a couple of miles out of town. Here the sea empties itself endlessly into subterranean tunnels or *katavothrai*—but there is no fear of the Adriatic running dry for scientists have shown that these tunnels are in fact the ones that eventually supply water to the underground lake at Melissani.

There are good sandy beaches at Platis Gialos, just south of Argostoli, and across the bay at Lixourion, the island's second city. Yachting facilities are also good.

Lixourion can be reached by road, but the frequent ferry services across from Argostoli are far quicker. Although it is of historic interest, it is not as attractive as its neighbour. There is a folk museum, but the archaeological museum in Argostoli is the chief source of information about Kefalinia's past.

For the future, it would seem to me an island that could well be about to be 'discovered' by the tourist industry. It has direct air links with Athens as well as a network of ferry services, and when the airport is upgraded shortly to international status it could well herald a tourist invasion. That will not spoil Kefalinia, for the island, with its wide bays, dramatic mountains, fertile plains and green forests, has plenty of room for everyone and is ripe for development.

Visitors will be interested in the village of Kastro, which stands among the ruins of churches, monasteries and houses; the mediaeval village of San Giorgio, which once held 15,000 inhabitants inside its hefty ramparts; and, across the Plain of Krane, the picturesque village of Assos. At Mazarakata, excavations at a number of Mycenaean tombs have produced a haul of beautiful vases, most of which are in national museums. No doubt, these are all the excursion centres of the future.

The farthest south of the Ionian islands, off the coast of the Peloponnese opposite Kilini, is Zakinthos, also known as Zante. Like Corfu, it boasts a mild climate and soft scenery dotted with vineyards and olive groves—a combination that moved the Venetians to christen the island 'the flower of the Levant'. But Zakinthos also suffered heavily in the 1953 earthquake, and the modern buildings now scattered over the island seem to intrude upon the scenery rather than melt into it.

This criticism does not strictly apply to the main town, called Zakinthos too, where rebuilding has been in a modified version of the original Venetian style, the houses and spacious squares somehow reminding one of Rhodes Town. There are several good modern hotels, including the Strada Marina and the Xenia, and the charges for accommodation are very reasonable. A ferry-boat makes several daily crossings to Kilini.

For a comparatively remote island, Zakinthos is remarkably alert to the demands of the tourist trade. In the town the seafront is lined with cinemas, one of them showing English-language films during the summer and employing touts who roam the streets to inquire anxiously of visitors: 'Are you going to the English movie tonight?' Near the top of the hill dominating the harbour is the Church of Aghios Nicholas, which boasts a fine silver-framed, life-sized gold icon of the Virgin and Child, dating from 840. Restaurants in town are good and English is spoken in many of them; the surprising local speciality is goulash, and there is a good local wine that costs less than many soft drinks.

Roads in the north-west of Zakinthos vary from the bad to the non-existent, but it is worth hiring a local boatman to take you to the famous Blue Grotto caves. To the south-west there are good beaches, especially at Lagana. At the Bay of Keri there are some curious pitch springs, used throughout history by the islanders for shipbuilding. All along this coast there is good spear-fishing, and the strings of *tavernas* naturally specialize in seafood, especially delicious red mullet.

The island is popular with Greek holidaymakers—always a good sign. And it is an island which, somehow, tugs at the heartstrings. The people are glad to see you, and sorry to see you leave. Indeed, despite the frequency of the ferry services, it can seem as though the whole town turns out to wave goodbye on the day you set sail, and to call: '*Kalo taxithi.*' It means: safe journey.

4 THE SARONIC ISLANDS

You do not have to travel very far from Athens to reach your first Greek island. Salamis is just a 20-minute ferry ride from Piraeus, the port of Athens, while Aegina, only 16 miles offshore, is perhaps the first place where one can find the restful and even timeless air which is associated with the Cyclades islands to the south-east.

The seven-mile strait that separates Salamis from the mainland is the site of the sea battle in which the Athenians destroyed the Persian fleet in 480 B.C. Today those same waters are criss-crossed by modern ferries, many of them heading for Paloukia, the island's main port. A dry, rocky, crescent-shaped island, Salamis is said to have an unhealthy climate. It contains Greek naval installations. There is a good road to the island's capital, Koulouri, or modern Salamis, a couple of miles away, and en route one passes the site of classical Salamis of which few traces remain. Koulouri stands at the head of a deep bay on the west coast and is surrounded by extensive bungalow and villa developments which represent the fulfilment of the desire of even such city-dwellers as the Athenians to own a second, island home. Koulouri itself is not much more than a quiet fishing-port, with plenty of good restaurants specializing in shellfish and other seafood. An oddity of the bay is that, since ships from Far Eastern waters were laid up there 20 years ago, the Japanese pearl oyster has been found in the waters and is breeding there in its natural state. So check your lunch for valuables!

From Koulouri the road winds through olive groves and fields of vegetables, which are not too abundant on Salamis, before climbing pine-covered hills to the Convent of Faneromi, where a horrific mural of the Last Judgment depicts more than 3,000 damned and tortured figures.

Aegina, triangular in shape and more or less at the centre of the Saronic Gulf, draws many of its visitors from day-trippers and visiting yachtsmen. Aircraft arriving at Athens airport often fly over the island, and one cannot help but notice its greenness. It owes this to rich soil and plentiful well-water, which makes it good farming country; besides dairy products it produces pistacchio nuts, citrus fruit and juicy figs.

The main town, after which the island is named, is a pretty spot, with narrow streets and alleys lined by blue-domed churches and pink and white classical-style houses. The porous jars dotted everywhere perform the same function they always have performed—as water coolers. Open-air cafés and restaurants line the waterfront.

It is an easy bus journey of eight miles across the island to the Doric Temple of Aphaia, one of the most popular sites outside Athens and built in a splendid setting. En route one passes the not-so-beautiful thirteenth-century Omorfi Eliksia, or Beautiful Church, and the ruins of Paleohora, the mediaeval capital, which was built inland as a protection against pirates but which was plundered for its stone by the islanders themselves after it had been abandoned.

The Temple of Aphaia has a dramatic hillside setting surrounded by pine woods. There are local guides to explain the intricacies of the Temple, which is in a remarkable state of preservation and is unique in the islands. Along with the solitary fluted column that still stands in the town, which is all that remains of ancient Aegina, the Temple is a reminder that the island was once an important city-state in its own right and one which boasted a powerful fleet—a fleet too powerful, in fact, for the comfort of the Athenians, who could not accept a neighbour whom they spitefully described as 'the eyesore of Piraeus'. Athens conquered Aegina in 454 B.C., and after that the island's fortunes declined—although it did enjoy a brief return to its former glory in 1828 when, for a period of just under nine months, it was the official Greek capital.

The fishing-village of Aghia Marina lies just below the Temple of Aphaia. There are direct ferry links both to Piraeus and the town of Aegina, and the fine, sandy bay, backed by pine-clad hills, and the village's excellent *tavernas* have made it a popular holiday or weekend destination for Greeks and overseas visitors alike. Hotel and self-catering bungalow developments have sprung up around the bay. Boat excursions from Aghia Marina take in both the scenic beauties of the island, and its natural health-springs which are said to be good for rheumatism, arthritic conditions, and eczema.

Poros is separated from the Peloponnese peninsula only by a narrow channel, and it owes its name to this. The Greeks compare it with the Bosphoros, of which Poros is a derivation. It, too, is within easy reach of Athens, and is a popular weekend excursion. Although thickly wooded, it is not a particularly beautiful island, and nor is it a beach resort. Its popularity seems to be based partly on its picturesque setting, and partly because it is a relatively sophisticated island.

The town clambers prettily up bare rock, its pastel-coloured houses gazing across the limpid waters of the channel to its mainland 'twin' village of Galata. There are plenty of souvenir-shops and not-very-typical restaurants, but to swim one must take a boat to the beach below the eighteenth-century Monastery of the Virgin or the beach of the Neorion—neither of them memorable. The island's one road does manage to lead to some interesting excursion venues, among them the ruins of the Temple of Poseidon, and Poros is also used as a jumping-off point for exploring a not particularly accessible corner of the Peloponnese.

After Aegina, the most popular island in this group is probably Hydra. A long, bare, rocky and waterless island, Hydra has a surprisingly attractive port and a reputation for housing writers and painters.

It also has an air of prosperity about it, an air enhanced by the town's tall, nineteenth-century houses. These were built by mainlanders who fled to the island in the late eighteenth century to escape Turkish oppression. Because the island cannot support any other form of industry, these newcomers became merchants and adventurers, blockade-running during the Napoleonic Wars. With the profits they built their grand houses—but the houses themselves should not be mistaken for the outward signs of self-indulgence. On the contrary, a visit to one of them (which is sometimes possible during the summer—ask locally) will show that they were built to withstand a siege by vengeful victims or lawful dispensers of justice—and each contains its own bakery, store-rooms and huge cisterns to hold the island's most precious commodity, drinking water.

The advent of the steamship put Hydra back into the shadows as far as its mercantile role was concerned. But the big, sheltered port is a tourist haven, and the town itself is worth exploring for its unique architecture. Recommended are the none-too-cheap but nevertheless unusual tours on donkey-back—those patient beasts giving you a safe, if undignified, ride through the back-streets. Look out for the town's other principal architectural form: small white cottages with the doors, or window-frames, picked out in brilliant pastel shades.

The donkeys, alas, keep to the harbourside area. The town stretches on up the surrounding hillsides, and to reach these parts you must climb endless alleyways of steep steps. The climb is worthwhile, however, if only for the view and the escape from the slightly claustrophobic atmosphere below. There is an even better view from the monasteries on top of the island's mountain ridge, and you can hire a mule to go up there. The beaches are poor all over the island.

Hydra's principal rival in this area is Spetsai, which is growing as a holiday destination and is also a base for sailing holidays. It is a small, green, wooded island which, like its neighbours, can be approached either from Athens (up to five hours on the ferry, or two hours on a sometimes uncomfortable hovercraft) or by *caique* from the Peloponnese mainland. Once one of the most exclusive spots in Greece, Spetsai now has an air of faded elegance that is highlighted by its houses built in the Napoleonic era. The pretty town spreads inland up a slope, and high-rise buildings have been banned. The ferries arrive at the new harbour, but there are villas to let on the east coast facing the mainland, around the old harbour where they build and repair fishing-boats. Inland, the roads can be rough, and as there are only a handful of cars on the island there is no incentive to improve them. Transport is by horse and buggy, or in the one dilapidated bus that crosses the island to the fine beach of Aghi Anargiri. The beach is well equipped with *tavernas* and other necessities, and you can also reach it by boat from the main town. In fact, if you want to go swimming or sunbathing you don't have much choice, for Spetsai's shingly beaches are generally poor.

The island is a good base for boat excursions and for exploring the Peloponnese. And the pleasant, roomy town of clean white houses makes Spetsai the most suitable of the Saronic islands for a prolonged stay. I am glad to report that, although it is becoming a holiday island, it remains unspoiled. Perhaps this is because there is little to see or do inland, and the local people—all 5,000 of them—still have limited horizons and their feet firmly on the ground. This latter fact can be inferred by the fact that there are 60 churches on the island—one for every 83 people—and all of them are in every-day use.

Finally Kithira, off the southern coast of the Peloponnese, celebrated as the birthplace of Aphrodite, is another island with a growing number of visitors, particularly Greeks themselves. Greek-Cypriots may raise objections when they are taken to Aphrodite's

1 *Above* Hydra's pretty harbour, which can be visited on day trips from Athens.

2 *Left* Corfu seascape, one of the many quiet bays on this popular holiday island.

3 *Below* Corfu Town. Parisian-style Colonnades are a legacy of the French occupation of the island.

4 *Above* A corner of Spetsai, now a fashionable resort, seen from an old monastery.

5 *Left* The Temple of
Aphaia on Aegina,
dating back to the fift
century B.C.

6 *Below* Mosaic in the
'House of the Masks',
on Delos.

7 *Above* One of the famous windmills on Mykonos, the most popular holiday island in the Cyclades group.

8 *Below* The Terrace of the Lions, on Delos, where five marble lions still stare blindly across the ruins of the island's former glory.

9 *Left* One of the most
familiar sights in Greece
and its islands is the
bearded and robed
village priest, or 'papas'.

10 *Below* Typical
Cycladic architecture,
on Tinos.

11 *Left* The huge
Church of Panaghia
Evangelistria on Tinos,
where pilgrims go to see
the 'miraculous' icon.

12 *Below* Almost like
icing sugar! Rooftops
near Kastron, on the
island of Sifnos.

13 *Above* Just stone and whitewash—yet Greek islands always look clean and well cared for.

15 *Right* Looking across the circular bay of Santorini from the clifftop town of Fira. The bay hides the volcano which destroyed the Minoan civilization.

14 *Left* Rocky Amorgos, one of the lesser-known Cyclades islands and a religious treasure house.

16 *Above* The rooftops of Skopelos, the most beautiful island in the Sporades group.

17 *Left* A courtyard and fountain in Rhode Town, the best preserv· walled mediaeval town in Europe.

18 *Left* An ornamental doorway in Lindos, the famous beauty spot on Rhodes.

19 *Below* The view across Patmos, where St John wrote the Revelations.

20 *Left* Drying sponges on Kalymnos which, with Leros, is the centre of the Greek sponge-fishing industry.

21 *Right* The port of Kalymnos, one of the loveliest of the Dodecanese islands, with its backdrop of mountains.

22 *Above* A Roman mosaic, which shows Hippocrates, in the museum on Kos—the island on which the 'Father of Medicine' lived and taught.

23 *Above* A fortress-crowned hill on Astipalea, one of the smaller Dodecanese islands close to Rhodes.

24 *Below* A frieze from classical times, and depicting hunters, which can be seen in the museum on Thassos.

25 *Above* Part of Sir Arthur Evans' reconstruction of Knossos, Crete.

26 *Below* Site of the Minoan Palace at Malia, Crete.

27 *Above* A typical Greek Orthodox Church interior: this one is in the
Monastery of Preveli, Crete.

birthplace, however, for in Cyprus coach-tours still stop at a spot near Paphos to show visitors the place where Cypriots say the goddess arose from the sea.

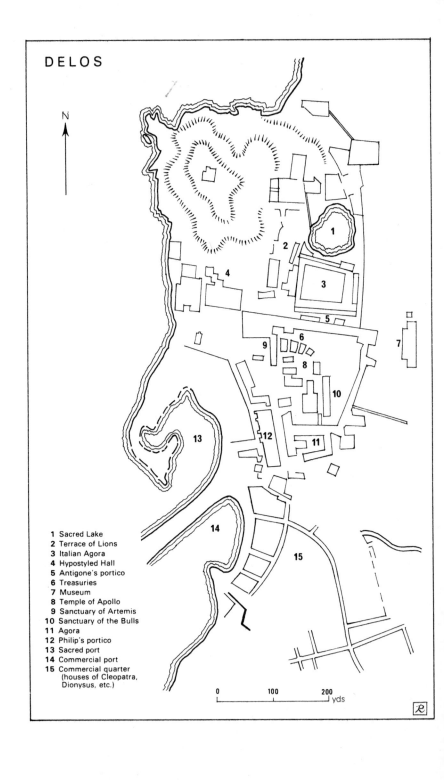

DELOS

N

1 Sacred Lake
2 Terrace of Lions
3 Italian Agora
4 Hypostyled Hall
5 Antigone's portico
6 Treasuries
7 Museum
8 Temple of Apollo
9 Sanctuary of Artemis
10 Sanctuary of the Bulls
11 Agora
12 Philip's portico
13 Sacred port
14 Commercial port
15 Commercial quarter
   (houses of Cleopatra,
   Dionysus, etc.)

0   100   200
                    ┘ yds

5 MYKONOS AND DELOS

For many visitors the island of Mykonos epitomizes the Greek islands in general and the Cyclades islands in particular. The crowded harbour with its guardian windmills, the busy seafront lined with bars and *tavernas*, the maze of back-streets, and the peculiar Cycladic architecture of chunky, cubist white-washed houses with tall, fretted chimneys—these are the things that attract tens of thousands of visitors to the island every year. Many of the visitors are the 'beautiful people'—young, well-heeled, trendy and, I regret to report, often not at all beautiful in either appearance or habits.

For the Ancient Greeks, nearby Delos—the centre for Greece's most popular day excursions—epitomized a way of life. A small, rocky piece of land not much more than three miles long and half a mile wide, Delos was once the religious centre of the Aegean and the island around which the other islands in the Cyclades group were gathered. That it has kept much of its magic, and certainly its air of timelessness, is shown by the fact that seeing Delos is still one of the highlights of any visit to the Cyclades.

Greek legend, ever inventive, says that Delos was once a floating island on which Leto, a mortal who had taken Zeus as a lover, sought refuge from the jealous and vengeful Hera. There are a number of these 'floating island' stories in the Aegean, and they may stem from the explosion of Santorini when huge masses of light volcanic material may have collected together on the surface of the water and taken a very long time to disperse and sink. Delos, the legend says, was caused by Zeus to take anchor at the spot where it rests today, and there Leto gave birth to Apollo. Be that as it may, Delos, the 'island of light', was a religious, artistic and commercial centre of the Ancient Greek and Roman worlds, and the island, with its famous marble lions, is now a tourist centre.

Travelling by *caique* from Mykonos, it takes a little over half an hour to reach Delos. Because Delos was sacred, birth and death were not allowed to occur there—and the *caique* passes Rheneia, where pregnant women and the old and sick were taken, on its way to Delos. Ahead lies Delos itself, with its safe, natural harbour and crowned by its sacred mountain, the conical, 386 feet-high Kinthos. The natural harbour and the legend of Apollo's birth made Delos important to the Ancient Greeks, who ranked it with the mainland sites of Delphi, Olympia and Epidaurus as a sanctuary. Choirs of young virgins appeared there at the annual religious festivities (a tribute which must have particularly pleased the rapacious Zeus), and during the Athenian ascendancy pilgrims arrived in Delos from all over the known world to see the processions and games, or to consult the oracle there. The island developed into a city, full of temples and grand houses, and it reached its peak when the Romans granted it tax concessions that enabled it to develop as a trading-centre between East and West.

The glory did not last. As the Roman Empire broke up, so Delos became the centre of a struggle that rolled back and forth across the Aegean. The islanders fled, or were slaughtered, and the great buildings were demolished. Pirates moved in to make it a base, and scavengers from other islands looted it for building materials. It was not until 1873 that excavations began to uncover ancient Delos once again, and these excavations continue to this day.

One needs at least three hours, and a detailed guide-book and map, to tour the ruins of Delos properly. You cannot spend the night there, so if you do not see all that you want to in a single trip you will have to return. The Sacred Harbour, the Sanctuary and the Gymnasium are all relatively well preserved as is the Sacred Way and a number of small temples and shrines. A map makes some sense of the litter of broken columns and fallen pieces of sculpture poking out from among the myriads of wild flowers. But the five marble lions, symbols of strength, are something one does not miss or forget. They stare blindly across the ruins of Delos's former glory.

You can still find the Sacred Lake, full of greenish water and looking rather like a large septic tank. And there are some interesting finds in the small museum, although this appears to open only intermittently—a fate it does not share with the inevitable souvenir- and refreshment-kiosk attached to it.

The island's old commercial quarter, a few hundred yards to the south of the Terrace of the Lions, is in a better state of repair. Here the ruins are of residential houses built in the Hellenistic and Roman periods, and although the size of the houses varies according to the importance and wealth of their owners—the houses of merchants, shipowners and bankers being the largest—the style does not. All the houses have a central courtyard with the main rooms leading off it, and an underground cistern for storing water on this dry island.

Frescoes on the walls, and mosaic floors made up of tiny coloured pebbles, often depict scenes from the owner's life, although there are religious and mythical themes too. Particularly noteworthy is the House of the Dolphins, where a remarkably well-preserved mosaic depicting dolphins and fish with intertwined tails has given the house its name. Just as remarkable is the House of the Masks, where the protective wooden floor-coverings are lifted to reveal a variety of mosaics, including the famous theatrical masks and the superb representation of Dionysus seated on a panther's back and holding a staff and a drum. This latter mosaic has immense grandeur, life and vitality, and is one of the high-spots of a tour of the island.

Below the House of the Masks is the well-preserved Theatre of Delos, dating back to 300 B.C. Its tiered rows of seats, including special high-backed seating at the front for important officials, meant that the Theatre could hold 5,500 spectators. And finally there is Mount Kinthos itself, a worthwhile claimant on any visitor's time, for it offers a fine view of the surrounding islands. The hill, easily climbed by a long flight of steps, turns out to be not nearly as steep as it looks from below.

Apart from the accessibility of Delos (although you can go there on excursions from Tinos too), it is hard to justify the popularity of Mykonos. True, it is linked to Athens both by ferry and by regular air services that use the island's tiny and inefficient airport, but it has suffered badly from its popularity. By day it is noisy, crowded and expensive, a proprietary brand of soft drink costing up to twice what you would pay on one of the neighbouring but less popular islands. During the evenings, the cruise ships call there, crowding together outside the harbour and disgorging hordes of passengers to add to the congestion in the maze of narrow back-streets that were originally built in that fashion to mystify raiding pirates. One could not find anything more un-Greek: a plethora of western-style restaurants and night-clubs, with the discos blaring out the latest transatlantic pop music and the clientele of late seeming to include a larger-than-usual proportion of homosexuals.

Goodness knows what Peter, the famous pelican who has made his home in Mykonos harbour and spends his days wandering forlornly among the beached fishing-boats on the shingle, makes of it all. And yet, especially outside the main season, there are compensations.

For a start, the town itself really is beautiful when you take the crowds away. The maze of streets is a delight, and even if many of the houses now sport a boutique in the front room the chances are that the occupants still hang freshly caught squid outside to dry in the hot sun. Persevere, and you will find your way across town, past the toy-town churches in infinitesimal squares, to the towering windmills and the town's 'other' seafront, the row of old houses called Enetia (Venice), which somehow turns its back on the ocean.

There are flowers everywhere—unusual on a seafaring island. Mykonos, alleged by mythology to be the burial-place of the Centaurs, was an infamous pirate base until as recently as the eighteenth century, but the islanders put their ships to more lawful use during the nineteenth-century struggles for Greek independence and are proud of their history. And the men of Mykonos have matched their adventures at sea with the endeavours that they have put into turning their bare, stony island, which is perpetually short of water, into a productive place; every possible scrap of land is cultivated, and every possible source of energy has been put to work. Even those graceful windmills still turn lazily all summer long.

The result is delightful, for outside the main tourist season Mykonos presents a picture of an island that is truly treasured by its people. The whitewashed houses are warmed by the orange colour of the shutters, picturesque carved wooden balconies, myriads of dovecots, and countless pots of flowers. The tiny pink- and blue-domed churches—360 of them, on an island of less than 4,000 people—are typically Greek. The two most famous beaches, Megali Ammos and St Stephen's, are clean and unspoilt—perfect for both water-skiing and underwater fishing—and have very adequate bars and refreshment facilities (try *amygdolata*, the almond paste of the island). There is an erratic bus service to the beaches.

At the ferry terminal, on the edge of town, scores of old women wait to tout rooms and lodgings, while their menfolk wait with barrows to transport visitors to this somewhat makeshift but usually clean accommodation. There is a good, if somewhat crowded, range of hotels too—try the first-class state-run Leto, set in a magnificent walled garden and with lovely rooms enjoying a superb view across the harbour. And after a siesta, before the 'beautiful people' come out to play, shop in the lanes and alleyways for dresses made in Mykonos fabrics, and other local handicrafts. Look out for the island's architectural gem, the Paraportiani, four chapels built on the site of an old fortress near the quay and now comprising one church. And if you are not staying at the Leto, the view from the Athens School of Fine Art, which occupies the town's highest point, is to be recommended.

There is also a good archaeological museum in Mykonos, containing many of the finds made on Delos: eighth-century-B.C. geometric Cycladic vases, funeral vases of lead and marble, Roman statues, jewellery and household articles. Of special interest are a marble statue of Heracles, and relief scenes of the Trojan horse.

It is as well that there is so much to see and do in the town for, apart from the trip to Delos, excursions are few and far between. There are short sea-trips to the islet of Dragonisi, about a mile offshore, where the crumbling cliffs have formed caves now inhabited by families of seals. On land there is a pleasant drive to the island's only other village, Ano-Meria, with its attractive monastery, or one can make the two-hour ascent by mule to the summit of Mount Aghios, at 1,195 feet the island's highest point.

You will have to return to the harbour for dinner—and that is a hazard. True, the little town looks at its best with the last rays of the sun striking gold off the houses, and with the pink oleanders and scarlet hibiscus aflame in every corner. But you will need to choose carefully from among the variety of restaurants and *tavernas*. The restaurant at the Leto is quiet and respectable, if unadventurous, but you may fare better in one of the *tavernas* used by local folk. There you may not entirely escape your fellow tourists, but at least you will hear *bouzouki* music, perhaps be lucky enough to hear the songs and see the dances of the local fishermen, and eat the specialities of the island: lobster, shrimp, roast sucking-pig, *louza* sausage and peppery *kopanisti* cheese.

6 THE OTHER CYCLADES ISLANDS

An ultra-modern car ferry was waiting at Piraeus, the port of Athens, bound for the island of Naxos—and I was disappointed. Four years earlier there had been only a rather dishevelled steamer of uncertain age and temperament, with a captain to match. The trip then represented something of a challenge, for Greek island ferries appeared to go both when and where it suited the owner or the skipper. Timetables? They existed, of course, but you relied on them at your peril.

The new ship—it, too, is called *Naxos*—is very different. Sleek and efficient, it is so punctual that you can almost set your watch by it. It has to be punctual, for it does the round trip in a day, calling at the other Cyclades islands of Paros and Siros and stopping for only a few moments at each in order to load and unload its impatient cargo of vegetable-lorries, tourists' cars and jostling foot-passengers.

It is just not the same any more.

The ferry was paid for by the people of Naxos who wanted to improve both communications and tourist traffic. When you board it you know exactly where you are going, and that can be a disadvantage. For Naxos itself has also changed. Big and beautiful, with a pretty harbour, fine countryside, dramatically deserted marble quarries (one, at Flerio, even has a half-completed statue in it), and some of the best beaches in Europe, Naxos has become caught up in the merry-go-round of making a quick drachma out of the tourists.

'I,' announced the rather striking lady who was running one harbourside hotel, 'am one of the two most go-ahead people on this island.' The other go-ahead person was alleged to be a local excursions organizer, and if they were go-ahead then I would hate to meet any of the island's more backward folk. The hotel in question was sloppily run, and the only organized excursion I took ended abruptly when I discovered that my fare included the cost of ferrying one of the organizer's friends across the island by taxi—and sharing my seat with him into the bargain.

I complained vociferously to go-ahead person number two, and number one appeared mysteriously on the scene with her eyes flashing dangerously. 'Why,' she demanded of me, in a startling *volte face*, 'should we make ourselves slaves to tourism?'

Why indeed? Tourism might benefit if some of Greece's more dubious entrepreneurs made themselves slaves to something else. And the country would surely benefit. But fortunately there is another side to the Greek islands, and it still exists in sufficient quantity to ensure that the essential qualities of this part of the eastern Mediterranean—its unspoilt solitude, its simplicity, and its endless variety—can still be found and will continue to be available to the discerning traveller for years to come.

You will not, I suspect, find these qualities too easily on Naxos, for there are islanders who seem determined to get rid of them as soon as possible. And that is a pity, for when it comes to prospective tourist havens Naxos has everything.

The island is the largest in the Cyclades group—a beautiful island with which the poet Byron quite understandably fell in love. The town after which the island is named has a hefty port and seafront, and a pretty church on an islet in the harbour. But it gets less attractive as you move away from the seafront, for the town starts to climb up towards the palace of the Venetian dukes who made Naxos their headquarters when they dominated the area, and the narrow lanes are unattractive and claustrophobic. The palace itself forms the upper part of the town, while by the water's edge on one side a causeway crosses to the lonely ruins of the Temple of Apollo. These ruins have been partially restored, and the huge doorway is an emotive spot at sunset.

Back on the quay, there are plenty of good *tavernas* plying their trade under the stern gaze of Petros Protopapadakis, an Edwardian figure from these parts who was Greek premier in the early part of this century and whose statue dominates the port and landing-stages. Good accommodation is, as I intimated earlier, less easy to find than a good meal.

Organized tours are equally hazardous, but as the beaches around the town are not particularly clean, and the island itself is so beautiful, it is worth exploring. Taxis can be hired quite reasonably with three or four people sharing for the day. And there is lots to see.

The jumble of marble at Flerio, and at another quarry at Apollona, remind one of the part that Naxos played in the development of classical Greek art. The island had a stormy history too, having once been captured by the pirate Barbarossa. But today the green interior is evidence of successful farming. Beside the road, prickly pear flourishes, and often one finds the roads winding through thick olive groves.

The most popular trip is across the island to Apollona, 40 miles away. The road from the town twists through reed beds before climbing gently up to the fertile Plain of Livadi, which is intensely cultivated. You get a fine view of the Venetian Belognia Castle, and next to it the twin church of St John (to the left it is Catholic, to the right Greek Orthodox), before reaching the fortified central village of Halki, with its Venetian castle and cluster of Byzantine churches, many of which have good frescoes. The village itself is unspoilt, and the villagers welcoming. You can get refreshments there. Nearby is the beautiful village of Filoti, where the church of Panaghia has a fine sculptured steeple. Then the road goes to Finelia, with its panoramic views, and charming Apiranthos, which is famous for its Venetian mansions. Still climbing, one reaches Koronos, Skado, and the road tops 2,000 feet before dropping dramatically down to the idyllic setting of Apollona.

An alternative trip from Naxos town is south to Upper Sagri, dominated by the Byzantine monastery of Kaloritsa, and Lower Sagri with its Venetian castle. Or one can go north-west to Avlonitsa, where there are more Byzantine churches with good frescoes, and the grim castle of Apalyros. There are attractive *tavernas* at Koniaki Sangri, and folk-dancing in the main square at Kinidari.

Naxos's nearest neighbour is Paros, an hour away on the daily ferry and, although it is so close, an island which is in direct contrast to Naxos. Paros was once inhabited by Cretans, and was known as Minoa. Like Naxos, it was once famous for its marble quarries. But today it is earning a reputation as a particularly unspoilt and attractive holiday island with excellent beaches. The hippies got there first—a fact made clear by the stern notice that greets visitors as they get off the ferry at the main town of Parikia, which warns: 'Nudity is forbidden.' Not that nudity, or any degree of it, is likely in tidy, flower-filled Parikia, with its long sandy seafront lined with tiny harbours and occasional windmills. The hippies have gone, and the pretty, narrow streets of the town are filled with shoppers—not holidaymakers and souvenir-hunters but easy-going islanders with a ready smile. Motorbikes are the only hazard: the young men of Paros have turned them into a craze, and they weave noisily around you wherever you go, so that a shopping expedition is rather like walking across a fairground dodgem-track.

The town's most visited building must be the Church of Ekatonta-piliani—Our Lady of the Hundred Gates. There are not a hundred gates, of course, unless perhaps one counts all the arches, windows and other openings. The rambling building dates from the sixth century, making it the oldest in the Aegean, and it is fascinating because it is in fact three buildings rolled into one: the Church of the Virgin, the smaller Church of St Nicholas, and a baptistry. Seventeenth-century rebuilding work in the interior has made finding one's way around rather a puzzle, and it is important to climb up into the ancient triforium which is the church's most beautiful feature. Look out, too, for the fine stonework in the smaller church, and the 'walk-in' font.

There are lots of cheap *tavernas* to choose from in town, and a very well-run and inexpensive Xenia hotel just outside it. There is also some new self-catering accommodation nearby which can be recommended. Outside the town Paros is not as attractive as Naxos, but it does have superb beaches, especially the palm-fringed Aghia Irene Beach, about three miles from Parikia. There are also good beaches at Aliki and Drys, near the town, and at Marpissa on the other side of the island.

Expeditions include a visit to the monastery of Longovarda, where the monks still paint icons, and to the Village of the Butterflies, a wooded valley reached by donkey on a three-hour round trip from Parikia. Like the Valley of the Butterflies in Rhodes, the Village of the Butterflies is a summer home for countless amber moths which rest in the trees but disperse in multi-coloured clouds when a guide shouts or bangs the tree-trunks.

One should make the short crossing from Parikia to the island of Antiparos, either on an organized *caique* excursion to see the stalactite-filled cave on the Hill of St John, or by hiring a ferryman to row you across. It is an easy ride by mule up to the cave, and one which is recommended for the spectacular views it affords of the southern islands in the Cyclades group. A properly constructed staircase, and the installation of electric lighting, have made the cave both more accessible and more beautiful in recent years. Antiparos also has some very fine and usually deserted beaches, and makes an ideal picnic spot. Don't worry about your boatman: he will row back to fetch you when you open the door of the church opposite Parikia.

The Cyclades are divided geographically into three groups: the western, the central, and the eastern islands. Besides Naxos, Paros and Antiparos, the central group is completed by Siros, the administrative capital of the Cyclades. The main town and port of Siros, Ermoupoulis, was once the principal port in Greece, and even today its big shipyards look somehow out of place in the Aegean. But the town itself, built on two conical hills, is attractive, and as most ferry services stop there it is worth exploring.

Behind the seafront, with its inevitable *tavernas* and a comfortable 'B'-class hotel in the shape of the Hermes, lies the town's main square, complete with tiny kiosks selling everything from newspapers and sweets to the strings of *kombolaki*, or worry-beads, which Greeks spend hours twisting between their fingers. Incidentally, these kiosks, which are more usually seen on the Greek mainland than on the islands, double up as public telephone booths. This tree-lined square is traffic-free, and is a lively meeting-point for the locals on a Sunday evening, when a band plays there.

The two hills immediately behind the square divide the town. The first, Ano-Siros, which is covered with white houses, reflects the long Venetian dominance of the island and is principally Catholic. The second, Vrontado, is Greek Orthodox. Most of the houses in the town are of a better standard than one normally sees in the islands, and they often reflect Siros's Venetian past. They also reflect the traditional prosperity of the island, and on the roads out of town this becomes even more apparent, for some of the country villas are distinctly grand. I find Siros a particularly warm and interesting island, but strictly speaking it is not for the long-stay holidaymaker. If you do spend a day or more there, however, there are good beaches at Galissas, Della Grazia, Finikas, and Vari. The islanders produce a special local delicacy: Turkish Delight as delicious as anything that ever came out of Turkey.

The western group of islands are the ones reached first on a boat journey from Piraeus. The first island of any importance one is likely to see is Kea, only 12 miles off Cape Sounion and a notorious pirate hideout in the not-too-distant past. The only raiders that it attracts today are the spear-fishermen for whom it is ideal, but it also has quiet beaches, particularly on the north-west shore, and a peaceful atmosphere. The islanders produce a dark red wine, honey and tasty apricot jelly.

Next comes Kythnos, the original city-state, another peaceful spot given over to the rearing of sheep and goats. Loutra, one of the three villages, is the only thermal resort in the Cyclades, and its spring waters are supposed to bring relief to sufferers from rheumatism and arthritis as well as developing resistance against the chills of the winter to come. There are four good beaches, but visitors usually want to devote their time to watching one of the popular local festivals, based on pagan rites. The Greek Easter celebrations (which are *not* pagan, but purely religious) are unforgettable.

Serifos and Sifnos are a pair of islands rapidly increasing in popularity with visitors. Barren-looking Serifos appears unpromising at first, and this impression is continued when the ferry docks at Livadhi, the hot little circular harbour. But the island turns out to be charming. Livadhi has a wide beach of sand and shingle which arcs round the town, and there are a couple of modest hotels as well as lots of private accommodation. You will eat well at the Stamatis *taverna* along the beach.

Many visitors prefer to walk or catch the bus up to picturesque Khora, a mile from the port through fields of vegetables. Khora, a white village built precipitously on a spur of land, used to be a mining centre, but today the miners have gone. You may find a clean, cheap room to let in one of the village houses, but accommodation is in short supply. Getting a good meal in Khora may be equally difficult.

Back in Livadhi, there are good beaches within easy walking distance, particularly at Psili Ammos, which has very fine sands. Excursions may be taken to the Taxiarchon Monastery, which has a library of rare Byzantine manuscripts, and there is a tenth-century Byzantine church in the village of Panaghia.

Sifnos, about an hour's ferry-ride to the south of Serifos, comes as a surprise, for it is a fertile island with plenty of water and this, coupled with its superb beaches, makes it another contender for future tourism development. The boat docks at Kamares, on the island's least attractive west coast, where a new jetty has been built. The port has its own beach, and hotel accommodation, not to mention a pottery, but the restaurants and *tavernas* are poor except for one good fish restaurant.

So take the erratic bus service up the steep road that climbs the side of Mount Profitis Ilias, whose 2,939-feet high peak dominates the island. After a journey of about three miles one comes to the capital, Apollonia, its flat-roofed white houses rising in an amphitheatre on three terraced hills. There are four modest hotels to choose from close to the little town square, and rooms to let in many private houses. Apollonia is a very Greek town, with tradesmen selling vegetables from panniered donkeys. For a while there was a danger of its being taken over lock, stock and barrel by mainland Greeks anxious to buy holiday homes there. But they now have their holiday houses at Artemon, about a mile to the north. Artemon has one serious disadvantage in that there is no *taverna* there—but it is still worth the walk from Apollonia because, if you go as far as the windmills, you get a superb view across Sifnos.

From Apollonia, one can travel to the huge stretch of sands at Plati Yalo (literally 'broad shore'), the biggest beach in the Cyclades. Visit, too, the picturesque and now largely depopulated fishing-village of Kastro, the dramatic site of which was also the site of ancient Sifnos.

Gold and silver were once mined on Sifnos, and a wealthy past is apparent in the abundance of relics: temples, mediaeval churches, and a Venetian castle. There are Byzantine treasures in the church of the Sotiros in Apollonia. But, perhaps fortunately, the island either does not quite know what the tourists want, or else it does not want to know. Travelling by bus to Plati Yalo or one of the island's other fine beaches is always a hazard, if only because you may not get back again too easily. The main beaches have *tavernas*, and Apollonia even unbends sufficiently to run a disco in the summer months. But with those exceptions, entertainment is hard to come by unless you are willing to settle for *bouzouki* music.

'Kimolia' in Greek means chalk, so it is easy to guess how the bleached island of Kimolos got its name. The famous pirate Barbarossa made his headquarters on Kimolos, but today it is a very quiet spot with good beaches and several important archaeological sites. Tourist interest is mostly concentrated on adjacent Milos, which is where the famous statue of the Venus de Milo was discovered and from which, the islanders will remind you accusingly, it was removed to the Louvre in Paris. Milos is a horseshoe-shaped island, with its port, Adamanda, near the bottom of the crescent. The most important excavations are at Phylakopi, where traces of three successive cities have been uncovered dating from the early Minoan period. There are several fine beaches, including the one at Hivadolimni, which is noted for its seafood, but accommodation is sparse.

In the central group of islands, beyond Paros and Naxos, a sickle-shaped curve of smaller islands bars the way to Santorini: Amorgos, with its precious Byzantine icons and manuscripts, and a fountain in the Church of St George which has always been regarded as an oracle; hospitable Ios, said to be the birthplace of Homer, with its very typical Cyclades landscape and atmosphere; remote Sikinos; and rocky Pholegandros.

For scenic grandeur, Amorgos is second only to Santorini itself. It is a mountainous little island, with cliffs on the eastern shore that have been called 'the wall of Europe' on the theory that all to the east of them is Asia. Ferries call at the port of Katapola, from which excursions can be made to the magnificently situated Monastery of the Virgin, or Hozoviotissa. It is a very attractive trip, and the white monastery nestling among orange limestone cliffs is very picturesque.

Pholegandros, too, is famous for its cliff scenery. From the tiny harbour of Karavostassis, a mosaic path climbs up to a white Cycladic town perched between the walls of an old fort on the edge of a precipice—it is a difficult trip but worth doing.

Ios, an increasingly popular holiday island, fits in oddly among its neighbours. Dominated by the twin peaks of Pirgos and Megalo Vouni, both over 2,300 feet high, it nevertheless has fine beaches and a very modern atmosphere, and it has been 'adopted' by holiday-making youngsters.

Ferries call at the harbour of Ormos Iou on the west coast, close to the excellent beaches of Yialos and Milopota. A regular bus service links the port, the beach, and the island's capital, the village of Ios, which lies about half a mile inland. The village is a pretty one, full of tiny chapels (there are said to be 400 of them), and set in farmland dotted with windmills. But it has no hotel, and accommodation is limited to rooms in private houses, two beach *tavernas* that let rooms, and a beach campsite.

All this makes the island's popularity with the younger set a trifle mysterious. In recent summers, at the peak season, Ios has had to turn holidaymakers away. One can only assume that the secret lies in the island's ambience, in its lively yet relaxed atmosphere. There are day trips to Santorini, always a fascination, and ferry services around the island, too, to deserted beaches where nude bathing—officially banned in Greece, but apparently tolerated on Ios—is popular. Rooms are cheap when they can be found, music blares out all day long from the beachside *tavernas* (particularly where two are

competing against each other for customers), and the night-life is
lively due to the wide selection of discos. The most popular of these is
the Ios Club, which combines an early evening classical concert,
timed to coincide with the sunset, followed by a rather more regular
disco.

Santorini is dealt with in the next chapter, but one must mention
at this point its small neighbour, Anafi, the most southerly island of
the Cyclades group, which mythology says rose from the sea on the
orders of Apollo to give shelter to the storm-bound Argonauts. Archaeological sites on the island do in fact bear traces of the Apollo
cult, in another of those strange links between fact and fiction that
the Greek past continually manages to produce.

Finally, there are the eastern islands: Andros, Tinos and
Mykonos.

Wooded, hilly Andros, with sylvan scenery quite untypical of the
area, is the second largest of the Cyclades islands and has a thriving
fruit-growing industry. It is dominated by an immense Venetian fortress, and is developing a number of holiday resorts along its fine
beaches, although these are at present used principally by Athenians. The ports of Gavrion and Batsi have bus links with the main
town of Andros, which is on the cool east coast and has two good
beaches as well as hotels. En route, look out for the patterned stone
walls around the fields, unique to the island, and the mediaeval dove-
cotes of patterned tilework that date from Venetian times and are
also found on Tinos. Up-and-coming resorts include the tiny village
of Korthion, Palcopolis (which also has some archaeological
remains), and Sarisa—a village that also produces mineral-water
from a local spring.

Tinos has had a flying start as a holiday resort because it has long
had good hotel accommodation and all the other trappings of a tourist infrastructure—but, until recently, it was not the beaches that
were the attraction. For Tinos is the 'Lourdes of the Aegean', a place
of pilgrimage that grew up around the contents of the white marble
cathedral, Panaghia Evangelistria, which dominates the town.
Inside the cathedral is a jewel-studded icon discovered in 1822 and
said to be capable of working miracles. Pilgrims flock to the island on
25 March and 15 August every year—dates on which the island is
definitely a place to avoid.

But for the other 363 days of the year Tinos takes some beating.
Around the town, with its fine harbour, are a number of good

beaches. Behind it the land rises through terraces of figs and vines (Tinos produces both *retsina* and a non-resinated sweet wine) to the heights of Mount Tsiknia (2,340 feet).

The Tinos Beach Hotel, a 20-minute walk from town along a poor road, is one of the best holiday hotels in the Cyclades. Big and modern, and under the genial ownership of a gentleman delighting in the name of Captain Stavros, it is set in fine grounds and has plenty of good food and on-the-spot entertainment. But it is perhaps a little remote from the 'real' Tinos, which one might find in one of the town hotels such as the Hotel Asteria. There are also plenty of typical places to eat around the harbour, particularly the *taverna* attached to the Hotel Aigli.

There are 1,000 churches on Tinos—one for every 15 people. But even on this religion-conscious island there could be nothing to compete with the spectacular Panaghia Evangelistria (Our Lady of Good Tidings), which stands on high ground at the rear of the town, poking out from among the cypress trees like some enormous wedding-cake. Built of white marble, and including a convent among its buildings, it is a spacious, impressive and peaceful spot. Inside the big courtyard, a monumental staircase leads up to the church which contains a variety of priceless treasures. But the one that everybody wants to see is the icon, discovered by a nun in 1822 after a dream. The icon itself is not particularly impressive, but the gold and silver offerings that surround it are—representing, as they do, the hopes and prayers of hundreds of sick and suffering people from all over Greece who make the pilgrimage to Tinos in the hope of a cure.

There is a museum just outside the church, built in the island's dovecote style. From the town, buses run to most of the island villages. There is good bathing from the beach at Kionoa, while the picturesque villages of Arnados and Dio Choria are worth seeing. There are good views of the Cyclades from Xombourgo, and Ormos Panormou has a fine beach beside its small harbour.

All the Cyclades islands are served by ferries from Athens and connected *caiques* to the smaller islands. These ferries are very cheap, especially for those prepared to travel deck class (which is no hardship, and may even be an advantage in summer). But the services, except for those to the main islands, can be erratic, and anyone with a flight to catch in Athens should allow two or three days for a journey that should not take more than six or seven hours.

The reason is that the ferries are mostly privately owned, and operate on circular routes that can be changed according to the whim of the captain or the owner. What is worse, they also tend to ignore one another's existence. Ask on the quayside when the next ferry leaves for Piraeus, and you may well be told: 'The day after tomorrow.' Then, when it is too late for you to do anything about it, you may see a ferry-boat sail in, set down a few passengers, and set sail again in the direction of Athens. What the ferryman at the quayside was in fact telling you was that *his* particular shipping-line's next ferry to Piraeus is the day after tomorrow.

And that is not an end to the difficulties. Vessels invariably leave Piraeus on time, if only for reasons of prestige. But once they get out to sea they can be delayed, perhaps by the unexpected storms that churn up the Aegean in the spring and autumn or perhaps by mechanical troubles. To catch up with himself, a captain may well decide to miss out an island or two from his schedule, leaving his passengers standing helplessly on the quayside. You can get stranded, too, as a result of the very fast turn-round that ferries have at some islands; some skippers seem to think that a ten-minute halt is excessive, and anyone who has hopped ashore to buy cigarettes is quite likely to return to find the ship, and his luggage, sailing out of the harbour entrance. Add a big question-mark about Sundays, when some ferry services run but most do not, and it can be seen why those with a flight to catch should prepare for the worst.

But whatever the drawbacks as far as transport is concerned, the Cyclades offer all the delights of island-hopping with the comforts of proper accommodation and a varied diet. Cool winds temper the summer sun, and that peculiar white light that the islands have brings them a warm, colourful glow.

And even if you don't know at what time the ferry will finally reach the island of your choice, it doesn't matter. It is enough to know that you *will* arrive, and that the islands will be waiting.

7 THE MYSTERY OF SANTORINI

The clatter of the anchor-chain woke me at 3.30 a.m. After a long day ploughing steadily through the Aegean at a top speed of 14 knots, the ageing ferry on which I was making the crossing to Santorini had finally arrived at its destination. It had been as pleasant a day as one could wish for, as islands came and went, the sun shone, and with hardly a ripple on the water. And if the boat was seven and a half hours late in reaching its destination, nobody seemed particularly worried—least of all the captain and crew.

There is another, more accessible, anchorage on Santorini, but most ferry-boats—and all cruise liners—choose to moor at the foot of the cliff below the island's capital, Fira. There can hardly be a more dramatic landing-place in the entire Mediterranean, and getting to the top of the cliff constitutes an adventure in itself. First, clutching your luggage, you have to clamber down into the tenders that ferry passengers ashore from the bigger vessels. Then, at the harbourside, donkeys and mules wait to carry you and your cases up the 587 steps—numbered in case anyone should disbelieve the tally—to the town itself. You haven't ridden on a donkey or a mule before? Nor have most of the other western European and American visitors to the island, but it is not as hard as it looks and there is no other way to reach the top—especially if, like me, you arrive in the middle of the night.

Arriving at such an hour means that it is not until next morning that one appreciates what you, and the donkey, have achieved in reaching the top: you have climbed the crater of a volcano. For Santorini is just that: the tip of a vast underwater volcano, 37 miles across, the edge of which has crumbled to let in the sea. The huge circular bay in which the ships moor is in fact the very heart of the volcano, and it is far from extinct. Although the water is many hundreds of feet deep, the strange, black island of Nea Kaimene arose in the centre of the bay between 1711 and 1712, and a sister island disappeared in 1868. There have been frequent earthquakes, the most recent in 1956 when half the buildings on the west coast were destroyed.

It is this tumultuous past that has made people suspect that Santorini is all that remains of the lost 'continent' of Atlantis. These claims have been given weight both by the fractured collection of historical facts and other evidence referred to in Chapter 1, and by the work of Professor Spiros Marinatos of the Athens Academy, who until his recent death was in charge of the archaeological excavations at Akrotiri, on the southernmost promontory of Santorini, where since 1967 a Bronze Age town of some 30,000 inhabitants has been slowly dug out of the pumice. Whole streets of two- and three-storey houses, many with staircases and the remains of wooden door- and window-frames, have come to light and now shelter under a vast roof of corrugated iron. In archaeological terms, however, investigations have only just begun, and there are indications that Akrotiri may soon rival even Knossos, on nearby Crete, both in size and interest.

Fira itself is a pretty town of white houses clinging to the edge of the cliff and tiny blue-domed churches that look as though they are made of icing-sugar. The view over Santorini and its neighbouring islands is superb, and for much of the year the area is bathed in the sparklingly clear sunshine peculiar to the Aegean. There are a couple of hotels of which the Atlantis is the best, but many houses in the town and in outlying districts offer accommodation. Except in the hotels, the food is the usual *taverna* fare and not always as good as in many other parts of Greece. To drink there are the famous Santorini white and rosé wines, which taste like the home-made wines that they are but carry a compensatory kick; beware of ordering them in hotel restaurants, however, because there is a price mark-up of more than 100 per cent.

Except for the obvious shape of the vast crater, it is hard to connect the Santorini of today with the events of the past. But the mystery of Santorini is, in many ways, even more fascinating than the riddle of the Minoan civilization on Crete, with which it was undoubtedly connected. Was this island the 'lost continent of Atlantis'? Archaeologists seem to be coming round to that point of view, although the evidence is fragmented. One of the principal arguments against it is that Plato placed Atlantis firmly out in the Atlantic, a location given credence by the fact that Schliemann used similar legendary evidence to correctly find Troy. Plato, in fact, described Atlantis as 'an island situated in front of the straits which are by you called the Pillars of Heracles (Gibraltar)', and said that the island was 'larger than Libya and Asia put together'. The island of Atlantis was 'pre-eminent in courage and military skill, and was the leader of the Hellenes. But . . . there occurred violent earthquakes and floods; and in a single day and night of misfortune . . . Atlantis . . . disappeared in the depths of the sea'.

This story has encouraged archaeologists to hunt for the lost continent all over the Atlantic Ocean and even beyond. There have been theories that Atlantis was Morocco, while an occult suggested that it was in Nigeria. One explorer claimed to have seen the walls of its citadel on a submarine reef near Heligoland. Mexico, Peru, the islands of the Caribbean, and even Ceylon, have been identified as Atlantis.

But given Plato's skimpy geographical knowledge of the world as it then existed, and the fact that he was relating a story that had never been written down but which had been passed on from generation to generation through the centuries, opinion now prefers the theory that Atlantis was the Minoan empire based on Crete and Santorini—an island whose ancient civilization was obviously well advanced. This theory is lucidly expounded by Professor J.V. Luce in his book *The End of Atlantis*. Professor Luce calls upon extensive archaeological and geological evidence to show that there would have been plenty of warning of the eruption of the Santorini volcano, and suggests that the island was evacuated—which would account for the absence of human remains found in the excavations at Akrotiri. The eruption itself would have been immense, and prolonged if the example of Krakatoa is anything to go by. The dust from the volcano would have fallen in quantities far greater than even that necessary to make habitation, or agriculture, impossible over a huge area. Devastating tidal waves would have caused immense damage throughout the entire eastern Mediterranean, and aerial vibrations would have caused damage to buildings more than 100 miles away. Professor Luce suggests that the merchants from Keftia, the name by which the ancient Egyptians knew Crete, and presumably the refugees from Santorini too, suffered too greatly to rebuild what was the Minoan civilization. They gathered together what little they could salvage and set sail to find new homes. They would have followed the old sea-routes with which their captains and sailors were familiar: westwards to southern Italy and Sicily, northwards to the Cyclades and Attica, eastwards to Rhodes, Cyprus and the Levant, and southwards to Egypt. But they sailed no longer as masters of the sea and chief traders of the eastern Mediterranean. They were now exporting themselves, not their goods. Says Professor Luce: 'A remnant of this Minoan dispersion may have settled as far away as Tunisia where a tribe of "Atlantes" was known in the classical period. A remnant certainly went eastwards and settled in the coastal strip of southern Palestine, and were later known as Philistines. The prophet Amos refers to this migration and, interestingly enough, links the event with a description of vulcanism and inundations.'

So the pieces of the jigsaw seem to be falling together. Certainly Akrotiri is a major clue, and the buildings that have come to light as a result of the excavations by Professor Marinatos show a very advanced civilization: the delicate frescoes that decorated its buildings surpass anything else in the Mediterranean, including Crete and can be seen in the National Archaeological Museum. The work continues although not, alas, under Professor Marinatos.

As well as Akrotiri, it is important not to miss Kamari Beach—composed of black volcanic sand that makes every other colour, from fishermen's nets to visitors' bathing-costumes, look extraordinarily bright. There is an erratic bus service to the beach from Fira, but the bus is worth waiting for because the fare is only about one-twentieth of what the mercenary local taxi-drivers will charge you. But the most fascinating excursion of all is the 20-minute boat-trip to Nea Kaimene, a stunted, evil-looking island of black rocks and volcanic ash with only a few tufts of grass and one solitary bush growing on it. From the landing-stage it is a half-hour's climb up to the Metaxa Crater, which is still active. Blasts of heat still pant from the fissures in the rocks, staining the ground a sulphrous yellow and giving the crater the distinctive smell of a child's chemistry-set.

In many ways it is a relief to escape back to the light and lushness of Santorini and to make the now familiar climb to the top of the cliff on the broad back of a mule which contains, according to local legend, the soul of a sinner serving out his time in purgatory. The 587 steps are certainly an awesome punishment, but instead of thoughts of repentance the steep climb (impossible on foot if you have any luggage) brings only a sense of wonder as the view unfolds once again. The colours really are magnificent: black, pink, brown, white and pale green. The bare peak of Santorini's highest mountain, Magalos Aghios Ilias, rises to 1856 feet, but it never dominates so spectacular an island.

There is another excursion to the ancient city of Thera. You can take the bus or a taxi to Pirgos, and continue by taxi, mule or on foot to the monastery of Aghios Ilias, from whose terraces there are fine views, and then by taxi or bus on to ancient Thera. This occupies a rocky spine and was built on a terrace supported by massive foundations. There are several interesting ruins, including the tiny chapel of Aghios Stefanus, the Gymnasium, and the Governor's Palace. The *Agora* is particularly impressive and a wall-plaque outside one of the houses suggests that the Byzantine sense of humour was not all that different to that favoured in some places in the twentieth century. It depicts a phallus, and is inscribed: 'To my friends.' See also the Sacred Way, the Terrace of the Festivals, and the Gymnasium of Epheboi, with its extensive graffiti.

Also recommended is the trip to Oia, by bus, taxi or mule. The road follows the cliff on a spectacular route through white villages to the promontory of Skaros, the mediaeval capital of the island. Below Oia, which was ruined in the 1956 earthquake, there is the little port of Aghios Nikolaos from which one can get the boat across to Therasia, the islet which is another part of the Santorini volcano's rim, or, as perhaps one should say more accurately, Thira's rim.

Santorini has recently reverted to its ancient name of Thira, and at present both are in use to the bewilderment of locals and tourists alike. The problem could be settled by readopting the third name by which Santorini was once known, Kalliste, which means, appropriately enough, 'most beautiful'.

8 THE ISLANDS OF THE NORTH-WESTERN AEGEAN

Outside the main groups of islands are several more clustered in the northern Aegean. Of these the best known are the Sporades—the four islands of Skiathos, Skopelos, Alonissos and Skyros—which are only half an hour's flight from Athens and which also have car ferry connections to Evia and Lamia. They owe their popularity partly to this easy accessibility and partly to the fact that, on Skiathos in particular, a heavy emphasis has been put on the self-catering holidays that have become so popular in recent years as money has become harder to find.

The islands also have a languid atmosphere all their own which has undoubtedly contributed to their popularity as a holiday and excursion destination. But it is possible to have reservations about the Sporades. In many cases the people do not seem as friendly as elsewhere in Greece, and transport within the group leaves a lot to be desired.

Skiathos is the best known of the Sporades—a soft, green, wooded island with lovely beaches and an increasingly sophisticated tourist industry. The principal town, also called Skiathos, is built on two hills overlooking the harbour, and there is also a second harbour given over to boat-building. There are several hotels along its cobbled streets, and the town has a surprisingly modern air which it owes partly to recent development and partly to the fact that, until the nineteenth century, piracy was rife in this area and the townsfolk preferred to live in Kastro, built on an impregnable rock in the north of the island and still an impressive ruin. There is a museum, and a memorial to Rupert Brooke—a bronze 'statue of an ideal poet'—overlooking the sea.

From the town of Skiathos the island's only road wends its way to the Kalamaki peninsula where a number of Britons have made their homes in the considerable villa development there has been in that area. The road continues to the famous beach at Koukounares, which is one of the best beaches in the Aegean and is fringed with pine trees. Behind the pines the countryside is equally attractive, with an inland lagoon fronting fields and olive groves. To get to the island's other beaches—70 of them altogether—you either walk or hire a boat. The pebbled beach at Lalaria, with its crystal-clear water, is one of the best, and Krassa and Aghia Eleni also have their advocates. The undeveloped north coast of the island is harsher, and the sea often seems rougher.

There are two 'A'-grade hotels on Skiathos, and the Skiathos Palace at Koukounares is recommended. There are a handful of cheaper hotels, but you can rent a room in the town of Skiathos very cheaply indeed. Many of the beach *tavernas* are excellent, and *moussaka* is a local speciality. But several of the *tavernas* have also adopted the admirable practice of cooking anything a customer requires as long as they are given advance notice. So you can plan a gourmet evening meal in the morning—which is just as well because the buses stop running at 8 p.m. so you are unlikely to be going anywhere. Not that the people of Skiathos want you to go anywhere; they have a charming custom in which they present departing visitors with a sprig of basil or a gardenia, meaning, 'Please come again'. It is an invitation that many people find hard not to accept.

Where Skiathos leads, can Skopelos be far behind? The answer, surprisingly, is yes, for although rocky Skopelos is a very beautiful island indeed, with fine beaches, a colourful town in the shape of Chora Skopelou, and women who still often wear the picturesque native costume of embroidered silk skirt, short velvet coat with flowing sleeves, and a fine silk headscarf, the tourist invasion has not yet arrived.

Chora Skopelou, built above a semi-circular bay, is attractively situated and is notable for its distinctive architecture. The houses are painted in pastel shades of red and blue as well as white, and have grey slate roofs with the ridges picked out in white—a form and colour combination not found anywhere else in the Greek islands. There are a handful of small hotels, including a good Xenia, and some pleasant walks through the olive groves to a smattering of monasteries and convents. Dried plums are the island's speciality, and you can watch them being dried, then polished with the fingers, in late summer. The island's other port is Glossa, a pretty spot, thick with fruit trees and olive groves, with some fine views across to Skiathos and the smaller islets.

It is less easy to be kind about Alonissos and Skyros. Alonissos is a humid, oblong-shaped island given over to farming and fishing, and the islanders give every appearance of disliking visitors—an attitude one rarely comes across in Greece. It has some good beaches, and there are beach bungalows to let.

Rocky Skyros, which is harder to reach than the other islands, is strictly for people who do not mind roughing it, although the folk-art shops have a tempting range of hard-carved furniture. There is a popular Xenia beach hotel.

The Sporades lie off the coast of one of Greece's largest yet least-known islands, Evia, or Euboea. Separated from the mainland by only a narrow channel opposite Chalkis, it is generally treated as part of the mainland. It is a very long peninsula, stretching from Lamia in central Greece down past Attica and almost to the islands of Kea and Andros. It is separated from the mainland by the Euripus channel. This is usually about ten miles wide, but at Chalkis it narrows down to the width of a river, and there it is crossed by a drawbridge that can be raised to let ships through. The channel itself is famous for its inexplicable current, which changes direction every three hours or so; the mystery of why it does this is said to have so infuriated the philosopher Aristotle, that he eventually threw himself into it.

The island, if such it is, is largely mountainous, with some afforestation and a fertile plain. It is a popular retreat for Athenians, who can reach the island and cross to the Aegean coast in four hours by bus and even less by car. Chalkis itself is a pleasant town with a few hotels (try the 'A'-class Lucy), a Venetian castle, and the Byzantine church of Aghia Paraskevi which has, in its time, seen service as a Gothic cathedral. It is a hard drive, or an easier ferry-trip, to the spa of Edipsos, where the sulphur-springs are said to cure rheumatism, and there is a good resort complex at Gregolimano which is easily reached from the mainland.

South of Chalkis is Eretria, once the capital's rival but now a ruin. Eretria has a big range of bungalow complexes for holidaymakers. Further on is Karistos, another popular resort, and there are good beaches at Marmarion and Nea Stira. Kimi, on the east coast, is well situated and looks across to Skyros, to which there is a ferry service.

Wooded Thassos, the most northerly of the Aegean islands, is also a strong claimant for the title of the most attractive. Volcanic in origin, and almost circular in shape, it lies only about six miles off the coastlines of Macedonia and Thrace and combines a beautiful and varied landscape with fine beaches and considerable archaeological remains.

Gold, marble, timber and wine were once the staples of Thassos's industry and wealth. Today it is a growing tourist industry, as people discover that there is nowhere else quite like Thassos. The island is dominated by its 3,747-feet-high mountain, Mount Hypsarion. Down the mountainside tumble thick pine forests which, with the plentiful water, give Thassos its green, fertile air. Roads, apart from the circular coast road, are poor.

The main town and port, officially known as Thassos too, is known locally as Limin ('harbour'). It has a few hotels, although the main holiday developments are outside the town. But Limin itself is worthy of a visit, for it is built on the site of the ancient city of Thassos and archaeological sites and modern buildings are jumbled together. From the harbour a path follows the course of the old city walls— past the Chariot Gate and the Gate of Semele-Thyone to the Greek theatre (used by the Romans for wild-animal shows) and up to the triple-peaked Acropolis.

On the Acropolis look out for the Sanctuary of Pan, with its ancient and rather worn carving of the god piping to his goats. From here there are excellent views across to Samothraki and the mainland. A sixth-century-B.C. rock-hewn stairway leads back down to the ancient walls and to the Gate of Parmenon, the Gate of Silenus, the Gate of Dionysus and Heracles (patron gods of Thassos), and the Gate of Zeus and Hera.

The portico-bordered *Agora,* whose foundations have recently been restored, is worth visiting, and there is also a museum.

The island's best beach, Makri Ammos (the 'long sand') is a half-hour's walk from Limin, and there are also bus and boat services. It is here that the basis of Thassos's booming holiday industry has sprung up—aided, no doubt, by the easy accessibility to the mainland and the island's popularity with holidaying or weekending Greeks from the north of the country. There are a number of good hotels as well as bungalow developments.

Farther round the coast, at Limenaria, there is further development. But with excellent beaches all round the coast road, and guest-house accommodation available at virtually every village, there is plenty to choose from. The best beaches include those at Kali, Rahi, Panaghia, Pefkari, Pharos, and Potamia. At Pefkari, there is also a memorable evening view of the whole of the Mount Athos peninsula.

The only real excursion is the tour of the island, a trip enjoyed by many Greeks who take their cars across to Thassos for the purpose. But for once the Greeks may be missing out—for most visitors prefer the boat-trips operating from Limin and Limenaria.

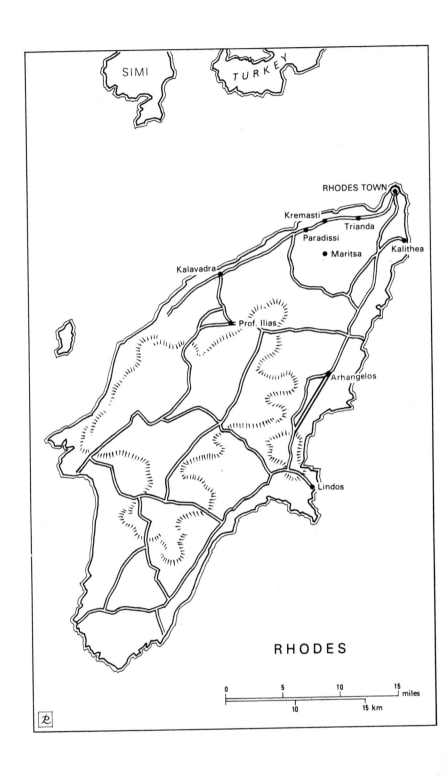

SIMI

TURKEY

RHODES TOWN

Kremasti

Trianda

Paradissi

Maritsa

Kalithea

Kalavadra

Prof. Ilias

Arhangelos

Lindos

RHODES

0 5 10 15 miles

10 15 km

9 RHODES

If you want to find the best holiday resort in any country, then find out where the locals go. That generalization is the advice of many travel writers, and for Greeks the favourite resort is Rhodes—the most southerly of the Dodecanese islands, off the Turkish coast, and favoured with an exceptionally mild climate in the off-peak and winter months. If you are Greek, Rhodes has the added attraction that along with the rest of the Dodecanese it is a duty-free island, with drinks, cigarettes, perfume and toiletries cheaper than anywhere else in the country. One in every six of the island's visitors is Greek.

Rhodes is also a popular port of call for cruise ships and has a growing year-round popularity with holidaymakers from all over Europe and, strangely, Japan. The Japanese go there to marry—an enthusiasm that local tourist officials find hard to place but which they think must be attributable to the legend that any woman climbing barefoot up the steep, rocky path to the Church of Aghios Tzambaki, a few miles outside Rhodes Town, then praying in the church, will experience no difficulty in having children. Rather than litter the hillside with Oriental pilgrims suffering from blistered feet, Rhodes has encouraged the Japanese to marry, or to have a Japanese wedding blessed, in churches in Rhodes Town or in the outlying villages—an idea the Japanese accept in sufficient numbers to necessitate a series of mass marriages every winter.

The Europeans go there for the sun, for Rhodes combines being known as the island of Helios, the sun-god, with being one of the most southerly points on the continent of Europe. From April to October there is usually uninterrupted sunshine, while the occasionally wet winters are broken up by long sunny spells when it is warm enough to sunbathe and even—if you are exceptionally hardy—to swim in the sea.

This is just as well, for the principal disadvantage of Rhodes is that there is little to do when the sun disappears. 'Come and see the night-life of Rhodes,' appealed the man in the minibus who was touting for one of his tours at one of the hotels I stayed in. 'You will find it very exciting.'

To be fair, he did try to make it exciting. But night-life is hard to find on the island at the height of the summer season, let alone in November. There was a meal (served with unusual speed) in a *taverna*, an energetic but somewhat confused exhibition of Greek dancing, a quick drive around the darkened Crusader city of Rhodes, and a visit to an otherwise empty night-club. Rhodes is short on discos and other gathering-places for the young and lively, and although one could go on—at additional expense, a not inconsiderable deterrent—to the casino at the Grand Hotel Astir Palace, most of the man's customers decided long before midnight that they would settle for an early night rather than a riotous one.

Rhodes, nearly 60 miles long and about 25 miles wide, is a lozenge-shaped island 12 miles off the Turkish coast. From Rhodes Town, which occupies the northern tip of the island and is home for about half of the 70,000 inhabitants of Rhodes, the mountains of the Turkish mainland loom large and magnificent. One used to be able to take a boat excursion across there, but Greco-Turkish relations are always sensitive and since the Turkish invasion of northern Cyprus in 1974 the Greeks have been particularly intransigent. When I asked about such an excursion, a tourism official advised me laconically: 'Forget it.'

The island's scenery is varied: Europe in miniature. No doubt this is responsible for the story that when God made the Earth, the crumbs of clay that fell off his fingers at the end formed Rhodes. Strangely the other legend about the island, that it rose from the sea and was given to Helios by Zeus because he had forgotten Helios in the division of the world among the gods, is nearer the truth; geological evidence suggests that Rhodes did indeed rise from the seabed in some vast volcanic disturbance millions of years ago.

The island has been inhabited since Neolithic times, and the Minoans built the first cities on Rhodes: Ialyssos and Kamiros. The Mycenaeans were next; then the Dorians who built lovely Lindos. It was not until 408 B.C. that Rhodes Town was built—planned by the islanders as a centre for the sea-trade at which they were adept. It was to grow into one of the Mediterranean's largest and most important cities in the Hellenistic period just before Christ's birth, and it is thought that the population then may have been 100,000—far greater than it is today.

But such a port was bound to be a prize that military adventurers could not resist. Rhodes has been overrun by a succession of Mediterranean conquerors, and the protection of Helios has proved to be singularly ineffective. It was not always so: in 305 B.C. a siege of the island was broken and, as a gesture of thanks, the islanders resolved to build what was to become one of the Seven Wonders of the Ancient World: the Colossus of Rhodes.

According to tradition, the Colossus bestrode the entrance to the present-day Mandraki harbour, in Rhodes Town. Mediaeval prints show him thus. The statue is known to have been made of bronze, to have towered 90 feet high, and to have been sculpted by Charis the Lindian. But it collapsed in an earthquake in 227 B.C. only 75 years after its completion, and the metal was broken up and sold all over the Middle East by Saracens who carried it away on the backs of 900 camels.

The harbour story is a pretty one, but the latest archaeological evidence suggests that it is incorrect. Contemporary reports state the Colossus could be seen from all five of the ancient town's harbours, and the only site from which this would be possible is the hill in the town on which stands the mediaeval Palace of the Knights. Moreover, some large edifice is thought to have been erected on this site at the time of the Colossus—so it seems likely that it was indeed a huge statue but that it never bestraddled the harbour.

Today, nothing more dramatic than a row of windmills, and two slim columns supporting statues of a deer and a hind, greet visitors arriving by *caique* at Mandraki harbour. The deer are the symbol of Rhodes, and commemorate the days when the island is said to have been overrun by snakes. The islanders consulted an oracle, who advised them to introduce deer on to Rhodes. This was duly done, and the snake population was virtually eradicated, although no one seems to be too sure about how or why the deer should have turned on the snakes. There are still wild deer on Rhodes, mostly in the quiet southern parts of the island, and snakes are reported to be few and confined to dry areas. Nevertheless, the womenfolk in country areas still wear knee-length goatskin boots which are peculiar to the island in that they have no left and right feet and that they are turned over twice at the top as a protection against snakes. The local costume also includes a long dress and a white scarf wrapped purdah-like around the neck and face as a protection against the sun in summer and cold winds in winter.

The Romans, arriving from Italy, were the first people to use Rhodes as a tourist resort, and both Cicero and Caesar are said to have liked to holiday on the island. In the Middle Ages the battles between the Saracens and the Crusaders raged around Rhodes, with both sides having possession of it at one time or another. A military order, the Knights of the Order of St John of Jerusalem, turned it into a stronghold, building on fortifications begun by the Byzantines, and their works were such that Rhodes Town is today the best-preserved mediaeval town in Europe. But finally the Turks took the island and held it until 1912, excluding Greeks from the fortified town at night, the punishment for being found in the town at night was death.

In these circumstances it seems surprising that the Greeks should have been able to retain their language, customs and identity for nearly 400 years. But keep them they did—and continued to do so after 1912, when the Italians took over from the Turks, and then on until 1948, when Rhodes was finally incorporated into Greece.

The island, then, has a rich and varied history, and this is amply illustrated by the wealth of monuments both inside and outside the massive turreted and moated walls of the Old Town.

For a bird's-eye view of the town, go out to the hill of the Acropolis, which today bears the very un-Greek name Monte Smith (it is named after a British admiral, Sydney Smith). There, sheep graze among the ruins of the Temple of Athena and the Temple of Apollo, and the local lads use for football practice a classical Stadium that would be hallowed ground anywhere but in Greece, where archaeological treasures are two a penny.

The Old Town can be approached from the landward side, where triple walls and a double moat made it impregnable, or from the town harbour where cruise ships and mainland ferries tie up close to formal flower-beds filled with hibiscus. The land approach is the most dramatic, for one must still cross one of the bridges leading to the three main gateways—a process that brings with it the realization of what formidable defences the Knights of the Order of St John of Jerusalem built for themselves.

The Knights came from the whole of what was then considered to be civilized Europe, and they were divided into seven Tongues, or languages. Each Tongue built its own two-storeyed Inn on the narrow, cobbled Street of the Knights leading down to the harbour, and each had its own sector of the city walls to defend. Visitors can follow in the footsteps of the Knights only on Tuesday and Saturday afternoons, when there are conducted tours of the ramparts.

The town finally fell to Suleiman the Magnificent in 1522, after a long siege by thousands of Saracen troops. But it was defended by only between 600 and 800 Knights, and such was their bravery that the Saracens allowed them to march out unharmed with full battle honours. The Knights left for Malta, which became their new head-quarters.

At the top of the hill is the Palace of the Grand Masters of the Order of St John, built in the fourteenth century as a fortress within a fortified city. A Grand Master was elected for life from among the nobles of the Order, and of the 19 who ruled Rhodes Town, 14 were French. Their Palace—the gardens of which today serve as the centre of an excellent *son-et-lumière* production in summer—apparently escaped unharmed in the siege of 1522, but the Turks did inadvertently destroy it in a massive explosion in 1856, when it was being used as a prison. It was entirely rebuilt by the Italians during their occupation of Rhodes between the two world wars, with the intention of using it as a royal residence, and its Renaissance lines blend oddly, yet somehow smoothly, into the mediaeval background. Inside, there is now an interesting collection of ancient mosaics and statues from the island of Kos.

From the Palace, the Street of the Knights tumbles down the hill, lined with the Inns of the various Tongues which can be identified by the bright marble coats of arms over their entrances. The even narrower side-streets are mysteriously arched, giving them a conspiratorial look—but the arches had a practical purpose in that they defended the buildings against the effect of earthquakes.

Each Tongue not only retained its own language but also favoured ethnic architectural styles. Thus the first two Inns in the street, those of Provence on the left and Spain on the right, are built in the Renaissance and Catalan styles respectively. Farther down the hill on the left, past the Chapel of the French and British Knights, is the Inn of France, another Renaissance-style building with dragon-headed gargoyles poking out from the roof. Next door, the Inn of Italy is a relatively plain building, although it does boast a beautiful wrought-iron gate which is a copy of the original.

The other Inns are those of Auvergne, England and Germany. All have been restored, the cost having been met by the governments of the corresponding countries of today. The fifteenth-century Inn of the Tongue of Auvergne, restored after the First World War and now an arts centre, is one of the finest examples of the Inns; it is the only one that can be visited.

At the bottom of the hill is the cloistered Hospital of the Knights, now an archaeological museum and containing a noteworthy 2,000-year-old statue of Aphrodite kneeling. In fact the Knights are thought to have had two hospitals, but the exact location of the second is a matter of some dispute.

The remainder of the Old City within the walls is a maze of picturesque little streets and alleys dotted with shops and broken up by pretty fountains and by tiny churches mostly converted into mosques during the centuries of Turkish domination. Turkish influence is still strong in the market-place atmosphere which prevails. Buildings of note are the Castellan's Palace, the Knights' commercial court which the Turks converted into a fish-market but which has now been beautifully restored, and the Mosque of Suleiman.

Perhaps it is because it manages to combine the ancient and the modern so gracefully, to say nothing of combining many cultures and influences, that Rhodes Town is one of the most attractive and unspoilt cities in Greece. The new town, with its hotels, restaurants and shops, contrasts happily with the old, and both the number of public parks and the fact that the sea is on three sides gives the town an unusual spaciousness.

Keeping it that way may necessitate a firm hand and a lot of common sense. Rhodes Town is full of prime sites, and developers have their eyes on them. At the time of writing the Hotel de Rhodes, once the grandest hotel on Rhodes and certainly one of the most beautifully and centrally situated, is an empty shell whose windows stare blindly out to sea. The reason: an argument over whether it should be restored or whether it should be pulled down and its grounds used for rebuilding. One must must hope fervently that the former view will prevail.

Some of the modern hotel designs are distinctly futuristic. The Rodos Bay Hotel, outside the town, is built up against a hillside and has its swimming-pool on the roof—a combination that gives it the appearance of something out of a James Bond film-set. The semi-circular New Olympic Hotel is perhaps even grander and, with superb rooms and a whole host of public facilities, represents excellent value for money. In town, the Grand Hotel Astir Palace is the best hotel—again with a great variety of public facilities (including a night-club, a 'pub' selling draught beer, and the island's casino) but, unfortunately, an 'international' menu which, when I was there, left something to be desired. The Plaza is a good 'B'-grade hotel, while even on so sophisticated an island it is still possible to find accommodation in private houses very cheaply as long as you avoid such 'in' places as Lindos at the height of the season.

There are marvellous walks, beaches and excursion sites within easy reach of Rhodes Town. The Moorish-style seaside resort of Kalithea, eight miles out of town, is the spa to which Hippocrates used to send the more affluent of his patients, and even today the waters are recommended for obesity, arthritis, diabetes and high blood pressure. On the hilltop of Philerimos, approached through a pine forest, one can wander through the third-century B.C. ruins and visit the subterranean Church of Our Lady of Philerimos, with its fifteenth-century frescoes, close to a small monastery. From the hill a 15-minute walk leads to the famous Doric fountain on the site of ancient Ialyssos.

The second ancient city, Kamiros, known as the 'Pompeii of Rhodes', is about 25 miles out of town on the west coast of the island. Built on the slopes of a hill, it has the remains of a Doric theatre sweeping down to the sea, and it is one of the most beautiful spots on Rhodes.

To reach it from Rhodes Town you pass a rather less beautiful spot that has none the less come as something of a relief to islanders and visitors alike: the new airport at Paradeisi, ten miles (or a 20-minute taxi-ride) out of town. I say 'relief' because Paradeisi, built beside the sea, replaces the old inland airport at Maritsa which suffered from the hazard of having a hair-raising approach between two steep hills. At certain times, usually in winter, the air currents around those hills created an upward draught that made it impossible for aircraft to land there, and pilots hated it. 'Maritsa was not so safe,' confessed the commander of Paradeisi Airport phlegmatically, while showing me proudly around his new charge. Paradeisi is safe and convenient, and an essential addition to the island's tourist trade; Maritsa has been turned into a race track.

But, although the west coast has its attractions, both ancient and modern, it is Lindos, on the east coast and about 35 miles from town, that draws the biggest crowds.

There are two roads to Lindos from Rhodes Town. Take the new road if you are in a hurry, but the old if you want to see Rhodes, for the old meanders its way along the coast, making little detours inland to tiny villages like Arhangelos, where the women wear the island costume and the men sit playing *tavli*, or backgammon. One particularly meandering stretch of road is known locally as 'the widow's curves'; it dates from the Italian occupation of the island when the military authorities decided to straighten the worst sections of road. They did this by compulsorily purchasing the land on either side of the road, but the stretch in question belonged to an attractive widow who decided to appeal to the troops' commandant and invited him up to her house. According to the islanders, who clearly revel in the story, the commandant duly went to the widow's house for dinner, stayed late, and did not return until morning. The nature of these all-night discussions can only be guessed at; suffice it to say that the widow's section of road remained curvy.

Beside the road, the olive trees grow thick and sturdy in the fields. In Rhodes the olives are picked earlier than anywhere else in Greece—when green first, then a second crop being taken when the olives turn black. The olives themselves are very rich, with one kilogramme of olive oil being presssed from only four kilogrammes of olives. Rhodes is a very fertile island, and many other crops are grown there too, particularly on the inland plains which are suitable for cereals as well as citrus fruit or grazing.

To one's left, the sea is a bright, cobalt blue. The east coast of Rhodes has the best beaches, for they are of sand rather than pebble. Regular bus services from town run all along this stretch of coast, and the best beach of all is about ten miles out at Faliraki, which is very safe for bathing and has a number of beachside *tavernas* offering seafood, refreshing drinks, and *bouzouki* music. There are three fine hotels here: the Faliraki Beach and Apollo Beach, both 'A' class, and a lower-graded but very good family hotel, the Faliro Hotel.

Beyond the hilltop church of Aghios Tsambika, with its occasional barefoot pilgrims, one must keep to the old road to reach Arhangelos, close to which there is the interesting fourteenth-century Byzantine Church of Aghios Theodorous, which has some very rich frescoes in excellent repair, an impressive screen, and a pebbled mosaic floor of the kind found in Lindos, which looks like a woven carpet. By the door, instead of the pay-booth and souvenir-kiosk now despoiling so many of Greece's prettier corners, a notice endearingly requests: 'We pray the visitors if they please to give each his penny for goal philanthropic.' Who could resist?

Along this road too, busy with tourist coaches whose horns blast the ear with the strains of *Never on Sunday* at the slightest excuse, is the recently constructed 18-hole Afantou golf-course—one of only three golf-courses in the whole of Greece.

But it is Lindos that most people want to see, and few are disappointed. Lovely Lindos is, perhaps, everything that a classical site should be. As attractive as the Temple of Sounion, and with an acropolis comparable in richness to that at Athens, it makes a dramatic landmark whether one approaches it by land or sea, with the ruins of the Temple of Athena Lindia catching the sun from their bold position on the promontory of Mount Mamari, the mediaeval fortifications of the Knights of the Order of St John of Jerusalem and later of the Turks hulking just below the top, and the modern, whitewashed village tumbling down the hillside.

The history of Rhodes is encapsulated at Lindos, for one can find there the works of Byzantines, Crusaders and Turks, as well as all the paraphernalia of a modern holiday resort.

Once separating two harbours, and today dividing two attractive and popular beaches, Lindos is said to have been founded by the apparently indefatigable Danaos and his family of 50 sons and 50 daughters after they had fled from Egypt. Certainly the site was occupied before 2000 B.C., and Lindos later became the most important city on the island with its people venturing abroad to found colonies near present-day Naples and in Sicily. St Paul is believed to have landed at the almost circular bay below the acropolis during a storm when he was on his way to Rome.

Today Lindos is a very pretty village of 650 people, its white houses clinging to the hillside, and its streets and courtyards pebbled with tiny black and white stones laid out in geometrical patterns. Here shopkeepers beckon passers-by into their spotless showrooms to sell Greek pottery, leather goods, and lace—a twentieth-century trade flourishing amid surroundings where the Byzantines and the Crusaders both built churches (the latter can still be visited) and where history has left a peculiar air of timelessness.

It is a steep climb up to the Acropolis, the steps shaded by almond trees under which old women sit occasionally working at, but more often hawking, their lace. On the first plateau, look out for the famous ship engraved into the rock which served as the pedestal for some huge and long-lost statue.

On the plateau of the Acropolis itself, ancient and mediaeval monuments stand side by side. First there is the Knights' Government House, an elegant and striking building, then the ruins of St John's Byzantine church. Beyond these, a broad central staircase leads up to the huge stone platform that was a base for the Doric buildings including the Temple of Athena. Only a handful of columns remain standing, but this is still an evocative spot which is lent drama by its magnificent surroundings and extensive views.

Below the Acropolis and the village, the beaches are big, sandy and safe, with plenty of *tavernas* offering refreshment. But for accommodation of a higher standard than the private rooms and villas of which Lindos has plenty, one must go outside the village. Lindos itself is protected against any further big development, so the Lindos Bay Hotel is a mile or two away at Uliha Bay, where it overlooks another good beach.

Beyond Lindos, the road to the southern end of the island quickly deteriorates, and it is true to say that the southern half of Rhodes is seldom visited by tourists. You will need a hired car to reach this area, but you will be rewarded with remote and empty beaches and hospitable villages.

Apart from Lindos, the most popular excursion on Rhodes is to the Valley of the Butterflies, a long, wooded, garden-like gorge below the 2,000-feet-high mountain retreat of Prophitis Elias and just over 30 miles from Rhodes Town. A local superstition, which says that the prophet will slay anyone cutting down a tree, has left this area unspoilt despite its popularity with tourists, and it is worth noting that even the organized excursions there are relatively cheap, with the three-hour round trip from Rhodes Town costing, for example, only about half what you pay for the hire of a donkey to climb the steps on Santorini.

The valley owes its popularity to the fact that, in summer, countless thousands of golden moths settle on the trees, where their colouring renders them almost invisible. Bang or shake the trees, however, and the air is filled with a cloud of moths which show black and red undersides and swirl around like confetti. It is a unique and unforgettable sight which, unfortunately, can seldom be captured satisfactorily by the camera.

Rhodes has been dismissed by many visitors as an island of limited tourist value. See Rhodes Town, Lindos, and the Valley of the Butterflies, they say, and you have seen it all.

But the Greeks who flock there find something else, and in future years I believe that its popularity will increase. Its 400 hotels already cater for 26,000 tourists a week, and that number will grow. For Rhodes has that admirable mixture of having all modern facilities on a relatively unspoilt island, an island where there is room to breathe and where traditional Greek hospitality has not been abused and therefore lost. It catches the best of the weather, and it is cheap. You can lunch or dine well at a really good *taverna*, such as Anixis, just outside Rhodes Town on the road to the airport, for about the same as you would pay for a hamburger snack in other European countries.

You will even be able to afford a bottle of wine with your meal—and Rhodes produces its own. I recommend the white Lindos wine, for which the vintners have conjured an adjective that no connoisseur had yet dreamed of; it is, they say, a 'privileged' wine.

10 THE OTHER DODECANESE ISLANDS AND THE NORTH-EASTERN AEGEAN

Because of its beauty Rhodes, the capital of the Dodecanese islands, is known as the 'island of flowers', and in this respect it differs from many of its neighbours, which verge on bleakness. Although tourists do now visit the smaller islands, travelling by *caique* and staying in the islanders' homes or in *tavernas*, the Dodecanese as a whole remains the least-known part of Greece to the outside world. The larger islands are developing a tourist infrastructure, with hotels or bungalow complexes, a variety of recreation and entertainment facilities, and ferry services to and from the mainland; but in the smaller islands strung off the Turkish coast the visitor will have no choice but to live as the islanders do and create his or her own entertainment.

Gaunt, parched Patmos, 106 miles north of Rhodes, perhaps epitomizes the other islands adjacent to the coast of Asia Minor, for although it has little to commend it beyond its blue skies and even bluer sea, it is a peaceful spot. It has an important place in history too, for in a bleak, purple porphyry cave, half way up a hillside, known today as the Cave of the Apocalypse, St John wrote the *Revelations*.

One cannot help seeing the island's other principal attraction, for it is impossible to miss: a monastery which, with its towers and battlements, looks more like a Norman castle than a religious institution. The monastery dominates the whole island, contains some priceless manuscripts and other treasures—including three paintings said to be by St Luke—and has superb views all around Patmos and across to Samos and Ikaria, which are best seen in the dawn light.

Just south of Patmos is Leros, its green valleys and vineyards separated from each other by rocky hills. There are two big bays, Gournas and Porto Lago, one on each side of the island, and on the north-west coast there is good bathing at the two seaside villages, where you can eat fresh seafood in the *tavernas* for your evening meal.

Leros and neighbouring Kalymnos are the centre of the Greek

sponge-fishing industry, and mountainous Kalymnos is particularly delightful because of its clear blue seas and the ancient traditions which the sponge-fishermen have preserved. There are special celebrations when the fishermen set off on their sponge-diving voyages just after Easter, and even more special celebrations when they return again five months later.

Kos, just off the coast of Turkey and a strangely elongated island, is the island of Hippocrates, the father of modern medicine. Hippocrates studied and taught on the island, and there is a huge fourth-century-B.C. statue of him in the museum of Kos. Islanders will also point out an elderly plane tree in the town, which they claim was planted by Hippocrates despite the fact that a plane tree seldom lives for more than 500 years. There is an imposing castle and several early Christian and Byzantine churches to see, as well as a number of attractive villages which can be reached by bus, mule or bicycle. The islanders will happily hire you a bicycle, which is a popular way of getting around on Kos; as it is a mountainous island, no doubt cycling is also very healthy.

Between Kos and Rhodes are a cluster of four small islands which lack any tourist amenities but make up for this by offering crowd-free beaches and extremely cheap accommodation and meals. They are Simi, praised by the ancients for its beauty; Halki, with just two tiny villages on it; Tilos, which used to produce famous perfumes; and Nisiros, a spa resort.

One of the smallest, and certainly the most remote, of the Dodecanese islands is Kastelorizon, just off the coast of Turkey and with a population of only 500. Castel Rosso, the red fortress which gave the island its name, is on top of a reddish-brown hill overlooking the village, and besides the castle it is worth visiting the remarkable Fokiali Caves. There is no hotel, but the islanders will be glad to put up visitors in their spotless homes and the beaches make excellent camping-sites.

All the islands mentioned so far hug the Turkish coast, but three islands further out into the Aegean are also included in the Dodecanese group. These are Astipalea, half way between Rhodes and the Cyclades group of islands, and Karpathos and Kasos which are half way between Rhodes and Crete.

Astipalea was once known as the 'island of fish', and it lies in deep fishing-waters. It is now famous for its delicious honey. It is a pretty but seldom-visited island, with a village of white houses distinguished by wooden trelliswork balconies, a number of wind-mills, a castle, and the big, rocky Maltezana Bay. Although it is officially part of the Dodecanese, Astipalea resembles the Cyclades islands in character, and is perhaps the misplaced thirteenth isle.

Beautiful Karpathos has a dual personality that may yet turn the island into a holiday resort in its own right. The southern part is covered with dense forests and cascading streams—a most un-Grecian style of scenery that acts as a backdrop for fine but deserted beaches. The houses on Karpathos are painted in the traditional style of the island, with the lower halves blue and the upper halves white, and local costume is still worn too. Here, perhaps more than anywhere else in the Aegean, old customs and traditions are faith-fully adhered to.

Tiny Kasos, tucked away below Karpathos and the last of the Dodecanese islands, is famous for its sea caves although, like its bigger neighbour, it also cherishes its ancient dress and customs which are resurrected for various local fairs. The village of Arvanitochori, with its charming stone houses, is split into two by a mountain stream that churns through the middle. There are good but isolated beaches, and visitors should also see the island's walls and the Mon-astery of Aghios Mamas and Aghios Georgios.

Besides the Dodecanese group, there are five other islands in the north-eastern Aegean which constitute part of what could be called 'Greece in Asia'. These are Limnos, Lesbos, Chios, Samos, and Ikaria.

Limnos is the most northerly and, with its russet-coloured earth, big sandy beaches, and pretty villages, one of the most attractive. It is the site of the ancient city of Poliochne, built before Troy, and the modern harbour at Moudro is the departure-point for boat excur-sions to Thrace, Thassos, Mount Athos, and unattractive Samothra-ki. In the other port, Mirino, the biggest attraction is the two cinemas, one of them an open-air one for summer use, where Norman Wisdom films have a large local following; there are no queues, though, for if the cinema is full the manager simply fetches more chairs from a nearby *taverna* rather than turn away customers.

There are hotels and some nice bungalow developments where visitors can stay, but the interior of the island provides some sharp reminders that tourists are still a source of surprise and amusement. A motorist driving across the island in a small car with an inflatable dinghy on top had the uncomfortable experience of watching the workers in the fields pointing and rolling about with mirth at the idea of a car carrying a boat. And meals in some restaurants can prove to be Turkish-style, with everyone eating from the same dish and snatching the tastiest titbits as quickly as they can.

Lesbos, the home of the poetess Sappho whose erotic poems describing the physical effects of love-making on the bodies of young girls were to give the island's name to female homosexuality, was also the home of another great lyric poet, Alcaeus, as well as being the birthplace of Aesop, the storyteller, and the wise man Pittacos. In about 600 B.C. the capital city, Mytilini, was one of the most advanced and civilized cities in the known world, and today it is still a sophisticated spot despite the marks that have been left there by a succession of conquerors.

It is an island of surprises, from the remarkably advanced urban planning of the ancient city of Thermi, where the streets were laid out in fishbone design, to the petrified forest at Sigri with its stone trees fossilized millions of years ago. It is also an island for the Greek gourmet—for on Lesbos, in the waterfront cafés, one can enjoy olives from the trees growing around the Gulf of Gera, fresh sardines and salted anchovies from the sea, and *ouzo* distilled in the southern town of Plomarion.

Mytilini has a Genoese castle in a good state of preservation, the remains of an ancient theatre and a large Turkish town, and a good museum. At Thermi, a spa town, the waters are good for rheumatism. There are attractive island drives through idyllic scenery, with worthwhile stops at Aghia Paraskevi (there are memorable 'name-day' celebrations here on the penultimate Sunday in May) and Erossos, where there are good mosaics set in the floor of the fifth-century Basilica of St Andrew. Thirty-six miles to the north of Mytilini is the artists' colony of Mithimna, with its Byzantine fortress and attractive shoreline and beaches. At Mithimna, particularly, one can see how Lesbos has partly thrown off its Sapphic connections and earned another name: 'Island of the Blessed.'

Chios, with its stunning beaches, has a direct ten-hour ferry-link with Piraeus and is, with Lesbos, the most frequently visited of this group of islands. It is also one of the ten places that claim to have been the birthplace of Homer, and modern scholastic opinion is that it has the strongest claim, although scholars do not differentiate between the villages of Kardamilia and Volissos, both of which claim him as their own. Apart from Homer, Chios's most famous sons are some of the big ship-owning families of Greece, and the island's naval traditions are such that a large percentage of its young men go to sea.

The island's capital, after which Chios is named, is a friendly little town crowned by a Genoese castle. Although the beaches are so good, getting to them can prove arduous as the roads are poor. It is worth persevering, however, to get to Nea Moni, where a mosaic in a monastery high in the mountains depicts the life of Christ and has few equals anywhere in Greece. South of the capital are the mastic villages where a gum collected in crystal form from the terebinth lentisk tree was the original chewing-gum. Today the crystals are more often made into a liqueur or into a sweet, white, sticky jam called *ypovrychion*, which is served by the spoonful in a glass of water. In one of these villages, Pirgion, the women still wear the native costume of a coloured fringed headscarf the colour of which varies with their marital status.

Ikaria, one of the lesser-known Greek islands, between Mykonos and Samos, has just been discovered by the tourist vanguard. Its main claims to fame are its pine trees and the strange goatskin bags—made from the complete skin of a goat and constructed without any stitching at all—which the islanders carry on their backs and in which they transport everything from animal foodstuffs to their own lunch.

The port is small and disappointing, with a stony beach and comparatively expensive accommodation. But catch the bus to the north side of the island and you enter another world. It is an arduous journey, a three- or four-hour trip over rubble roads and through scrubland and pine woods—a landscape that occasionally takes on the appearance of a setting for a Wild West movie. The journey's end is Evdilos, a fishing-village soon to be developed into a proper port. Twenty minutes' walk from the village is the mile-long Campus beach, which stands in front of a freshwater lagoon and is usually deserted. Connoisseurs complain, however, that the sand is gritty, and arguably the best beach on the island is at Yalliskari, a 45-minute drive from Evdilos. This four-mile crescent of sand is backed by pine trees and makes a beautiful if lonely spot.

Except in the main port, the villagers on Ikaria are still not used to tourists and the hospitality can be embarrassing. But in return for this hospitality, visitors must sometimes suffer the humiliation of being objects of considerable curiosity. Blonde girls are in great demand among village youths, who want no more than the prestige of having been seen walking or talking with them, while those with the complexion that often goes with red hair may suffer the amusing but undignified scrutiny which an English girl recently received from a rheumy-eyed fisherman at Yalliskari. After peering closely at the girl's features, the fisherman confided in broken English: 'You should go up into the mountains—there is an old woman up there who can fix your face for you.' Hastily grabbing her mirror, the girl was relieved to find that her only blemish was a sun-induced rash of freckles, a condition still looked upon as a deformity in some rural parts of Greece.

Samos, to the east of Ikaria, is also off the usual tourist-track and is never crowded even in midsummer. Travellers do not know what they are missing, however, because Samos is among the most beautiful of all the Greek islands. It is also one of the most fertile, and the overriding impression that one gets is of its greenness. Fruit and vegetables grow in abundance and cost next to nothing locally, while the grapes growing on the hillsides go into making a fine range of wines much in demand overseas—even in traditionally wine-producing countries. The dry white wine is best, and can be bought cheaply on Samos; sweet Samos wine is too sweet for most tastes.

Dominated by the almost Oriental shape of the 4,720-foot peak of Kerketeos and the Ambolos chain of mountains, Samos is a rugged island despite its fertility. But, unlike most other mountainous regions of Greece, the hills often give way suddenly to green, sheltered plains and valleys.

The capital, Vathi, is a town with a dual personality: modern buildings round the harbour give it a dull, listless appearance, but Upper Vathi, where terraced red-tiled houses climb above the water, is a pretty spot. The town beach at Gangou is clean but uninteresting, and most visitors prefer to head for the island's ancient capital, Pythagorion, an attractive port ten miles from Vathi and named after the famous philosopher and mathematician Pythagoras, who—although he has been dead for 2,500 years—survives through his theorem to haunt our schooldays.

There are two superb beaches at Pythagorion, and nearby can be seen the remains of the Temple of Hera, another of antiquity's Seven Wonders of the World. An out-of-the-ordinary excursion at Pythagorion is to the tunnel dug in about 500 B.C. to bring water through a hill. This tunnel, still accessible for part of its length, was never finished but is thought to have been planned so that it could be dug from both ends simultaneously with the engineers finally meeting in the middle—an extraordinary feat for its time.

There are good museums in both Vathi and Pythagorion, but a third museum in the town of Mytilenioi is perhaps the most fascinating because it contains a unique collection of the fossils of a number of very large animals unearthed in the surrounding countryside and including the fossil of the so-called 'monster of Samos'.

Despite the fact that it is off the tourist beat, Samos has good hotels as well as accommodation available in private homes and monasteries, with the latter compensating for an occasionally somewhat Spartan existence by superb views and cellars of rare old Samos wine which may be offered to visitors. Handicrafts, silk and pottery are good buys in the shops.

One of the less attractive aspects of this idyllic isle is, however, that because of its proximity to the Turkish coast it is a heavily manned Greek army base. The troops, who apparently have nothing to do for much of the day, make up for their inactivity by extensive manoeuvres, and these noisy affairs start promptly at seven a.m. to the discomfort of any late-night revellers staying nearby. A more amusing aspect of Greco-Turkish rivalry over the centuries is the explanation for the hundreds of monasteries that litter Samos: the Greeks, fearing a Turkish invasion, have not been slow to recall that the Turks traditionally respect religious ground—a category into which large parts of the island now seem to fall.

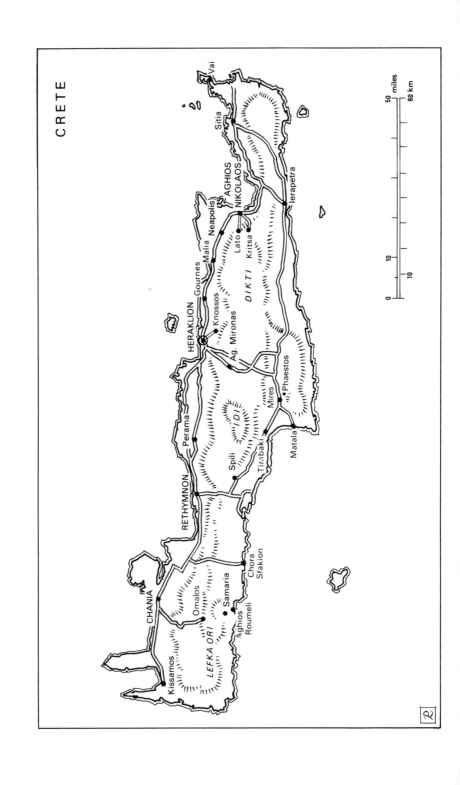

CRETE

CHANIA

Kissamos

LEFKA ORI

Omalos

Samaria

Aghios
Roumeli

Chora
Sfakion

RETHYMNON

Perama

Spili

I D I

Tirnbaki

Matala

Phaestos

Mires

HERAKLION

Knossos

Ag. Mironas

Gournes

Malia

Neapolis

AGHIOS
NIKOLAOS

Lato

Kritsa

D I K T I

Ierapetra

Sitia

Vai

50 miles

80 km

0   10   50

10

11 CRETE

The men of Crete have a motto, one they will relate to the visitor on every possible occasion. It is: 'Crete's weather is like its people—usually nice but able to get rough very quickly.'

Somehow that sums up both Crete and the Cretans. For Crete, the largest of all the Greek islands, is a rugged spot full of snow-capped mountains, appalling roads, huge sandy beaches, and stunning coastal scenery. And the Cretans have the same rugged individuality. Like Yorkshiremen in Britain or Texans in the United States, they are part of a nation with everything in the way of national pride and character that this involves: and yet they manage to retain their individuality and one is always aware that if they ever had to choose between Greece and Crete it would be Crete every time. They fought a long and savage guerrilla war against their Turkish masters from the Middle Ages right up to comparatively recent times, and when the Germans occupied the island during the Second World War they were never able to exercise full control over the Cretans, who fought on over the vastness of Crete's three great mountain ranges where a handful of men with local knowledge could hold an army at bay.

The shape of the Mediterranean means that Crete, besides being the largest island in the eastern Mediterranean with the exception of Cyprus, is on the same latitude as north-west Africa. Thus it is the most southerly point in Europe, and on the coastal plains it is blessed with warm sunny weather for most of the year. These late autumns and early springs contrast strangely with the snow that lingers until May on the Lefka Ori, Idi and Dikti mountains.

The Greeks wax lyrical about the place. One official tourist office's description of the island boasts: 'The trip to Crete is actually a pilgrimage. Every town, every village of the *megalonissos* (big island) has something to show, something special to tell. Wherever in Crete, the visitor will feel the warmth of home and the one to know Crete will never forget it. A trip to this island is a spiritual relax and a storage of cherished memories.'

A trifle effusive perhaps, yet impossible to contradict. Crete is an island with which it is all too easy to fall hopelessly in love.

Aghios Nikolaos, Crete's best-known resort, nestles at the foot of rugged mountains 45 miles from Heraklion, the island's capital, and it is as beautiful as Heraklion is ugly. 'Port' seems an inappropriate word to apply to Aghios Nikolaos, but it does have a harbour which widens into a lake in the centre of the town. Around the lake are clustered picturesque shops, houses and hotels. It is here, seated at tables by the water's edge, that the local residents spend the warm summer evenings indulging in their favourite occupation: watching the world go by. More accurately, they watch the rest of Aghios Nikolaos go by.

It was at this spot, on just such an evening, that I was introduced to Crete—and as Aghios Nikolaos is growing rapidly in popularity as an all-inclusive holiday centre my introduction will no doubt be shared by many British tourists. I had arrived in Heraklion with a friend, a Greek hotelier who had broken her ankle in Athens some days earlier. Because of this we were met by a chauffeur-driven mini at the airport, and the Greek driver had set out to prove that it was possible to cover the 45 miles to Aghios Nikolaos in less than an hour despite the fact that much of the journey is along precipitous mountain roads. We drove for a few miles along the flat, uninteresting coastal plain on the north of the island, through 'new' resorts like Malia (Ikaros Village is the best hotel), and then the road—since greatly improved—twisted sharply inland and upward. In a few moments we were hurtling along roads which at that time saw little traffic, through tiny villages, round tortuous bends, and along gritty unfenced lanes clinging to the mountainsides.

It was a hair-raising experience and it seemed to go on for ever. Eventually, as darkness fell over the mountains, we saw lights ahead and dropped down into Aghios Nikolaos, where the mini screeched to a stop outside a harbourside *taverna*. The driver looked proudly at his watch. 'Fifty-five minutes,' he said. 'But I could have done it faster if the lady had not had a bad leg.'

We sat down thankfully at one of the metal-topped tables outside the *taverna* and ordered *ouzo* and *mezethes*. Gradually, we relaxed. The *mezethes* (snacks of red mullet, slices of octopus, olives, goats' cheese, cucumber, and squares of toasted bread) arrived by the plateful in generous helpings which I liked to think were offered because I was a stranger, but which were more probably due to the fact that by her hotel developments my companion, Mrs Helen Nakou, has brought both fame and prosperity to this part of the island. The *ouzo*, the soft evening air, the jollity of the *taverna*, the shouted greetings between friends, and the holiday feeling imparted by Aghios Nikolaos all helped to soothe town-taut nerves and to emphasize the unique atmosphere of this big, remote, lovely, but sometimes harsh, island.

Rested and fortified, one can consider the other attractions of Aghios Nikolaos. Although it has a population of less than 4,000 it is the main town in the eastern section of Crete, and a wonderful touring-centre. It is an easy afternoon's drive, for instance, up to Kritsa, where the steep and narrow streets overlook Aghios Nikolaos and the blue waters of the Bay of Mirabello. On the way one should not miss the thirteenth-century church of Panaghia Kera, with its three aisles and fourteenth-century frescoes; the frescoes, considered to be the finest in Crete, have been lovingly restored by the Byzantine Museum in Heraklion. A stony track which no self-respecting motorist would use, but along which Cretan drivers roar quite cheerfully, leads from Kritsa to the idyllic site of the seventh-century Doric town of Lato.

Lato is a lonely place, as is another beauty-spot in the vicinity of Kritsa, the Katharo (literally: clean) Plain. A high plateau ringed by mountains, notable for its clear atmosphere and eerily total silence, the Katharo Plain is one of those rare spots where it is possible to imagine that you are absolutely alone on this planet.

A longer but more dramatic excursion is to Lasithi, and the Plain of the Windmills. A mountain road branching off the main road between Heraklion and Aghios Nikolaos climbs up to the high, fertile plain, where the sails of 10,000 windmills turn silently during the summer months, pumping water on to the potato-fields. This really is an extraordinary spot; it has the other-world atmosphere that one might expect of some forbidden land in a Victorian novel.

En route, you can make the two-hour climb up to the Diktaean Grotto where, according to legend, Zeus was born and where he was hidden so that he would not be eaten by his father, Cronus. The grotto was a place of worship during the Minoan period.

The sails on the windmills of Lasithi are turned by the north winds, or *meltemia*, which blow in Crete during July and August. The *meltemia* do more than water the Plain of Lasithi, however; they make the island's climate agreeable even during the hottest months of the summer, although they do tend to blow the sand around on north-coast beaches. A Cretan summer is a pleasant surprise after the sticky discomfort of Athens, 175 miles north.

A suntan comes very quickly indeed in these parts, and many holidaymakers in Crete like to spend a few hours on the beach and then spend the rest of the day touring. That is why towns like Aghios Nikolaos are developing as tourist-centres, for on an island 150 miles long, never more than 40 miles wide, and divided into four distinct regions by huge and almost impassable mountain ranges, it is remarkably difficult to get around. The roads can be bad, and it is a pleasant change to take an excursion by sea. From Aghios Nikolaos one can take a boat to the mysterious island of Spinalonga, once a Venetian stronghold and more recently a leper colony. Inside the huge walls of the fortress, Venetian and Turkish buildings remain. One could easily imagine that ghosts linger here too—creaking shutters hang loose and doors bang in the breeze in the streets where the lepers lived until the 1950s. The island is like a town from which the population has suddenly vanished, and the weeds sprouting from the floors of empty houses proclaim that nature's work of reclamation has begun.

Opposite Spinalonga is the tiny village of Elounda, whose inhabitants were once the deadly enemies of the people of Lato. But today the natives are quite definitely friendly—and they proved it by inviting me to a lunch party at long tables set up in the streets beside the tiny harbour. The Cretans do such things in style; under the benevolent gaze of the village priest, or *papas*, we consumed course after course, washed down with a sweet white local wine, and finishing only as the sun dipped below the horizon. It was a typical example of impromptu hospitality, and one which visitors can share even today in the more remote spots on the island. Such a welcome can be embarrassing, for the hospitality you receive can never be repaid, and even offering to pay for a round of drinks in return may be regarded as an insult. There is no answer to this problem and one must simply enjoy the hospitality and be grateful for it; as the number of tourists increases no doubt it will die away.

Elounda has become famous through a television serial, and book, *Who Pays the Ferryman?* It is a small but attractive village in a fine setting, with some simple accommodation, facilities for self-catering holidays, and a large choice of excellent *tavernas* specializing in fish dishes. For a really excellent meal, continue along the unmade coast road from Elounda to Plaka, where there is a very Cretan *taverna* offering no choice of food—you either eat what the proprietor has cooked (usually fish, and really excellent) or you go without.

On the road between Elounda and Aghios Nikolaos are three of Crete's best hotels: the Minos Beach, just outside Aghios Nikolaos, the Elounda Beach, and the Astir Palace, Elounda. All three are based on a series of bungalows and flats built around a central hotel complex containing such facilities as the reception area, restaurants, bars, lounges and discotheque; all three are expensive. At the Elounda Beach I was again a guest at an impromptu party to celebrate someone's 'name day' (Greeks attach great importance to this, and to feting someone called George, for example, on St George's Day rather than on his actual birthday). To the pulsating rhythm of a *bouzouki*, played without the dubious benefits of amplifying equipment, Voula, the wife of a local architect, and one of the musicians sang the light, amusing, yet strangely haunting Cretan *madinatha* songs, in which the two singers indulge in a 'conversation' made up of couplets played in the same, persistent tempo. To drink there was *raki*, the fiery local spirit that the Cretans deny has anything to do with the Turkish drink of the same name, and which they describe, straight-faced, as the 'Cretan Scotch'.

The demands of tourism have expanded Aghios Nikolaos rather considerably in recent years, and the mass of modern bars, souvenir-shops and discos fits uneasily into the picturesque port. But at least local *tavernas* are unspoilt, even if their menus have taken on a slightly international flavour with, in one case, Greek *mezethes* followed by such curiosities as 'omelete, marmelade, humburger, cheeseburer, hot roasbeef'. Still very traditional is the Doula *taverna* at the end of the quay, which in my opinion offers the best value in town, while the Creta Restaurant is also recommended.

From Aghios Nikolaos the main road from Heraklion continues, often following the coast, to Sitia, a pleasant port dominated by a Venetian fort and again enlivened by several attractive waterfront *tavernas*. There is a small and recently excavated Minoan palace at Kato Zakros, high in the hills above Sitia, and on the eastern tip of the island, near Paleokastron, can be found a forest of 5,000 palm trees sloping down to the sea—the only forest of its kind anywhere in Europe. The palm trees are said to have sprung from date-stones dropped by Roman soldiers, but whatever the truth of this legend they are now threatened by local farmers and monks who covet the agricultural land on which the trees grow; as a result the unique forest is shrinking perceptibly as more and more palms are felled and burned.

The other main town in eastern Crete is Ierapetra, a small port on the south coast but, with 340 days of sunshine a year, a strong claimant for the European sunshine record. Local residents wear short-sleeved shirts all year round, and claim that you can get a suntan at Ierapetra in January. Be that as it may, it is a lively and attractive town, with a fine beach shaded by feathery tamarisk trees, with good restaurants, *tavernas* and discos, and if one had to hazard a guess at Crete's 'resort of the future' Ierapetra would be hard to dismiss from the list of contenders. There is good bathing from the rocky coves around the town; the hippies who 'discovered' the town, and who gather there during most summers, are actively discouraged by the police. There are cottages to let—both traditional ones and the far more comfortable modernized variety—in the nearby village of Ayanis Koutsounari (it means 'big rock' in the Cretan dialect, and refers to the acropolis-like rock behind the village), which is so small that it does not even appear on many maps. You can eat well in Andoni's *taverna*. On the main promenade fishermen still mend their nets beside the road, while opposite, Spiros the barber, a man with an eye firmly on the future, has given up hairdressing in favour of running a shop full of souvenirs made from shells, coral, and other sea-bed oddities. Call in for a look around and Spiros will welcome you with a cup of Greek coffee and an assurance that there is no obligation to buy.

Between Sitia and Ierapetra you cross the narrowest part of the island and pass the early Minoan town of Gournia, the ruins of which are scattered over a lonely hillside. It is worth stopping and making the five-minute climb, if only because of the view.

From Ierapetra there is a mountain road across to Ano Vianos, a village surrounded by vineyards and olive groves. This is the real Crete, a hard country peopled by stern men who still carry rifles and by shy, self-effacing womenfolk. The Germans found it particularly hard to subdue these parts during the occupation of Greece in the Second World War, and guerrilla fighters who had fled into the mountains they knew so well used to emerge to attack German outposts. The Germans responded by indulging in wholesale retribution against the villages accused of harbouring guerrillas. There is a memorial at Vianos to victims of the occupation; other villages in

these mountains were completedly razed, or else saw the male in-
habitants taken as hostages and not infrequently shot. Even today,
German visitors cannot expect to be the recipients of traditional
Cretan hospitality; unlike so many other European nationalities, the
Greeks remember their grudges.

The road continues west to Mires and Tymbaki, past the beautiful
archaeological site at Phaistos where a Minoan palace second in importance only to the one at Knossos has been uncovered. Although
smaller and less imposing than that at Knossos, the palace is magnificently situated on a hill overlooking the rich Messara Plain, with
the bulk of the Idi Mountains, often snow capped, looming majes-
tically to the north. There is a tourist pavilion and museum nearby.
A short distance from Phaistos, at Aghia Triada, are the ruins of
another small Minoan palace thought to have belonged to a local
nobleman and again superbly sited.

From Tymbaki, a main road runs east and north to Heraklion,
and although the island's modern capital city is not a place that can
be recommended for a holiday, it cannot be missed if only because of
its crowning attraction: Knossos.

Even if it were not for the archaeological excavations at Knossos,
three miles south of the city, Heraklion would not be without interest, however. The fifth largest city in Greece, it is worth touring to see
its Venetian fortress (Crete is littered with them), its mediaeval
walls, and the Turkish market-place. The Morosini Fountain and
the Venetian town hall should also be seen, and everything is set
against a magnificent mountain backdrop. The Atlantis Hotel is the
most civilized in town, and you can eat well opposite at the Castro
taverna. But despite these attractions, Heraklion's very layout can
make it seem a dull, lifeless city, and the most important calls must
be at its Archaeological and Historical Museums.

The Archaeological Museum is the largest in Greece, with 23
rooms containing a wealth of beautiful exhibits representing the
various periods of early Cretan and Minoan civilization. There is a
priceless collection of gold cups, bronze daggers, jewellery, and in-
geniously shaped pottery; while the dazzling frescoes suggest that
when it came to graphic art the Minoans were about 3,000 years
ahead of their time.

In the Historical Museum there are displays of Cretan national
costume and representations of a typical Cretan home.

But it is Knossos, and its reconstructed Palace of Minos, which tempts almost every holidaymaker in Crete as well as the thousands of cruise passengers who make shore excursions to the site. Because the ruins are so extensive and so complicated—a fact that may have given rise to the legend of its labyrinth—you need to visit them with both a guide and plenty of imagination. The archaeologist Sir Arthur Evans did his best to bring Knossos to life, and paid the penalty for it by suffering a barrage of criticism for having gone too far with his reconstruction attempts. But the reconstructed parts of the Palace, with their blood-red pillars and the triple-storeyed Grand Staircase, bring reality to a site that would otherwise be almost meaningless to the layman. Other things not to miss are the various royal apartments decorated with their famous murals; the extensive and advanced sewage system; the armoury; the royal tomb; the restored Throne Room; the Hall of the Double Axes; and the Queen's Palace complete with its advanced (and still intact) plumbing system.

The interpretation of this immense archaeological site is, of course, open to considerable argument, as was stated in Chapter 1. As the years go by, the case that Evans made seems to get weaker, while Evans himself is shown as something of a pedant. Be that as it may, a combination of half a day at Knossos and half a day at the Archaeological Museum in Heraklion do give a fascinating insight into the civilization that is 5,000 years old. To tour Knossos properly takes several hours, and it is only fair to say that after hearing so much about it many visitors are disappointed. But it is important to remember just how old Knossos is, the fact that the Palace was at the heart of a city of anything between 30,000 and 100,000 people, and just how far ahead of their time the Minoans were culturally. Go to Knossos with an open mind and a little imagination and you will come away enriched.

The western half of Crete is wilder than the east and much less frequented by tourists. The main north-coast road runs 60 miles west to Rethymnon, Souda, with its large military base, and the old island capital of Chania.

Rethymnon is a pretty Venetian port that somehow manages to look as though it is still suffering from the visitation by Turkish pirates who burned it in 1571. Once fortified, it still has vestiges of grandeur. It also has a reputation of being the intellectual centre of Crete. But tourists will see it as an attractive town with rows of pretty houses often decorated with iron balconies. *Tavernas* ring the small fishing-harbour, while ferry-boats use a bigger and far less attractive harbour. The Venetian influence is strong; apart from the Venetian Fortress, the 'Fortezza', and the Venetian Loggia, look for the Venetian Niche with its coat of arms and a Venetian inscription at 35 Emmanuel Bernardou Str., the Venetian Niche at 44 Arcadiou Str., the facade of a Venetian building at 46 Arcadiou Str., the Venetian 'Arimondi' fountain, beautifully decorated with a Venetian coat of arms and lions' heads at Platano's site, and the four Venetian gates.

In the purple mountains above the city, at Arkadi, is one of the most emotive spots in Crete: the seventh-century monastery where the nineteenth-century running battle between the Cretans and their Turkish overlords reached an appalling climax on 7 November 1866. During the fighting a large number of Cretan men, women and children had taken refuge in the monastery, along with 1,000 monks. A large quantity of explosives was stored in the monastery, and when a strong Turkish force laid siege to the building the Abbot Gabriel had to make the awful choice between surrender (and probable slaughter) or using the explosives to destroy the monastery. He chose the latter, blowing up not only the monastery and its defenders and refugees, but an estimated 3,000 of the opposing Turks. The incident is still commemorated every year as a national holiday in Crete, and it also gave rise to the motto which is still a Cretan password: 'Freedom or Death.'

There is another strange, but perhaps less dramatic, memorial to the fighting between Cretans and Turks to be found in these mountains. At Vryses, a turning off the coast road leads south across the island to remote Chora Sfakion, one of the spots where the menfolk still favour the traditional Cretan costume of braided jackets, cummerbund, baggy trousers, and knee-length boots. The Turks, and the Germans after them, both found themselves involved in bloody battles when they tried to subdue this area. But one battle in particular resulted in a very odd after-effect.

Near Chora Sfakion is a Venetian fortress, the Frangokastello, or Frankish Castle, which the Turks decided to turn into a stronghold of their own and where they carried out extensive repairs. The repairs seemed likely to benefit their adversaries more than themselves, for by 1828 Cretan revolutionaries had seized the Castle. Under the command of Pasha Moustafa, a strong Turkish force was sent to recapture it, and a Cretan rebel force 386-men strong was ordered to abandon the building rather than battle against impossible odds. The Cretan leader, Michalis Daliannis, decided to ignore the order, and he and his men locked themselves inside the Frankish Castle to await the Turks. There was a long and savage battle, and the defenders and the attackers died to a man. And ever since that day, the Frangokastello has witnessed a strange phenomenon that still has not been satisfactorily explained.

Every year, on a day in the second fortnight in May, a little before dawn, when the sea is calm and the atmosphere peaceful, a long row of apparently human shadows, dressed in black and carrying bright weapons, walk or ride on horseback across the plain near the castle, as though they were taking part in military exercises. The phenomenon lasts for about ten minutes, and has been witnessed by hundreds of people standing on the Castle ramparts. But attempts to approach the mysterious figures have never been successful, and they always vanish without trace.

Because they appear early in the morning the Cretans have named these ghostly shadows the 'Drosoulites', or 'those of the dew'. Scientists say, unconvincingly, that the phenomenon is a reflection, or mirage, of a camel-train or military exercises on the adjacent coast of north Africa. But the local people will tell you that the Drosoulites are the shadows of Michalis Daliannis and the 385 Cretan fighting-men who died with him on that very spot a century and a half ago.

Chania, the former capital of Crete, is also its most beautiful city. It began its era of prosperity in 1252, when the Venetians took it over and decided to extend and rebuild what had been a small, cheese-making town. By the seventeenth century it boasted a fine harbour, strong fortifications, and the Kastelli, or old city, on a hill above the harbour. The Turks turned it into the island's capital, and it retained this honour when the island was eventually united with Greece. As a result, it still has many of the grand eighteenth-century buildings that were used as foreign consulates, complete with extensive gardens and avenues of palm trees. Indeed, these gardens, and the town's general air of greenness, have given it the nickname of the 'garden city'.

Today, Chania is two towns: the Kastelli and the other old quarters, and the sprawling new town. On the east side of the Kastelli, the Venetian harbour is dominated by the lighthouse at the end of the breakwater, which can still be climbed and which provides a superb view of the town. Not too many Venetian structures have been preserved, but part of the old walls are still intact and are worth seeing, as is the bastion of Schiabo Lando. The local tourist office occupies the old mosque of Hassan Pasha which was built in 1645. The most popular restaurants and *tavernas* are those around the old harbour, which is a gathering-point for the town's people in the evening. The colourful market is also worth visiting. Stay at the greatly underestimated Chandris Hotel, a short drive outside the town.

Chania is separated from the huge natural harbour of Souda Bay, now the town's ferry-port and an important naval base, by a pine-covered neck of land leading to the Akrotiri peninsula—a maze of lanes given over partly to the military and visited principally for its memorial to the Cretan statesman, Venizelos. There are several good bathing-beaches to the west of Chania, between the city and Maleme, which was the scene of some of the heaviest fighting between the Germans and Allied forces during the 1941 Battle of Crete. The western end of Crete is seldom visited by tourists, and the roads can be very bad, but you can drive across the mountains to Paleochora, where the bathing is excellent.

The most popular excursion from Chania, however, is inland—up on to the precipitous White Mountains and across the marshy Omalos Plain to the head of the 14-mile-long Gorge of Samaria, one of the largest crevices of its kind in Europe and a challenging expedition for the fit and adventurous. It is safest to walk the Gorge as part of an organized two-day excursion from Heraklion, so that there are no return transport problems.

There is a tourist pavilion at the head of the Gorge and the rocky climb down to the Libyan Sea takes about six hours. For much of the route one has to follow the bed of a stream, and this means that the Gorge is impassable in the rainy season or in spring when the snows on the White Mountains are thawing. It is best to go on an organized excursion, if only because of the logistics of getting to and from the Gorge. You need solid footwear, although the climbing-boots that many German hikers seem to adopt for this walk are totally unnecessary. I have seen a young British girl walk the Gorge in high-heeled platform-soled sandals, although she did so at the price of a fair selection of blisters. A notice at the top of the Gorge warns walkers that this beauty-spot is a protected area for wild flowers and animals—the rarest of the latter being wild *agrimi* goat that used to be found all over Crete but can now be seen only in the Gorge of Samaria. The stream is protected too—it supplies water to the settlements at the bottom of the Gorge and they prefer it if you have not washed your feet in their drinking-water.

The path down the Gorge is a testing walk right from the start, when hundreds of steps cut through woodland take you down to the level of the stream. Then there is a spectacular walk to the deserted village of Samaria, which is where the walking really begins to get hard. Fortunately, some enterprising locals wait there with donkeys to rescue the faint-hearted, but it is worth continuing the walk as the path cuts down into a very deep crevice until the rock walls rise sheer above you for hundreds of feet, cutting out the sunlight. At one point the gap narrows to less than nine feet and the rock walls—known at this spot as the 'iron gates'—seem about to crush you. Elsewhere the path is wider, with thick vegetation and bright wild flowers. In this, and in similar, smaller, less well-known gorges along the south coast, you come close to the real Crete.

Eventually, walkers emerge at the remote village of Aghia Roumeli, where there is a welcome *taverna*, and where a decision has to be taken on how to get back. You can telephone Chora Sfakion and hire a *caique*, and look at the site of ancient Tarrha on the outskirts of Aghia Roumeli; you can take the coastal path to Chora Sfakion, which passes the Chapel of St Paul built on the spot where St Paul is said to have come ashore on the island; or you can begin the long, hard climb back up the Gorge. The latter is not recommended.

The fact that such expeditions on Crete are hard and hedged with transport difficulties, however, perhaps adds to their charm as well as protects the island's remoter attractions from the ravages of the tourist hordes. The Cretans intend to keep it that way. Local bus services are fine along the coast, but beware of those in the mountains: village services run down into the main towns in the morning and back again in the afternoon, for the convenience of shoppers instead of tourists. Catch an afternoon bus up into the mountains, and you will have to spend the night there.

And this is as it should be. Crete could be a candidate for tourist despoliation. Already Heraklion's crowded airport cannot deal with the daily crush of tourists arriving in summer, and you are doomed to a long queue before you get through immigration and collect your luggage. Car hire prices have rocketed—partly, no doubt, due to the wear and tear wrought by Crete's rough country roads, but due also to the unprecedented demand. And the souvenir-shops are no longer the place for a bargain-hunter: in Heraklion you will pay £5 or more for the tiniest of sponges, and other popular local purchases—with the exception of surprisingly stylish local shoes—are equally expensive.

But Crete is big enough to take all this in its stride. It is an island to savour, a place where you learn a little, leave, and then return to learn more. It is an island of dreams, an island where, perhaps more than anywhere else, Greece lives up to all its expectations; an island where you can explore when the mood takes you but where you will probably spend most of your time just lying in the sun, making plans but doing nothing.

12 FOOD AND SHOPPING

The menu in the popular Greek island holiday resort was of the new, international variety. Holidaymakers, a few restaurants seem to have decided, will never have the courage to adopt the Greek tradition and go into the kitchen and inspect the food as it is being cooked. So they take advantage of a comprehensive mass-produced menu with prices written against those dishes which are 'on'. The menu is in Greek, of course, but the publishers have helpfully printed a translation below each item. Unfortunately, this translation can cause even more confusion—and choosing a meal remains as difficult as ever. Thus it was that I read with interest that the cover charge on my bill would differ according to whether I had had a paper 'narkin' or a linen 'narkin'. I passed over 'red chaviar' in favour of 'small suids stuffed' without any problem but was then faced with choosing a main dish.

'Brains salad' did not appeal, nor did 'stuffed spleen (Moroccan way)'—and 'calf's donge' seemed definitely to be avoided. 'Tender bowles' caused advance warning of impending internal discomfort.

Eventually I ordered 'grilled andricot steak', 'fiener schnitzel', and a little 'lettouce salad'. I passed over 'pouting' in favour of 'blue Dadish cheese'. At least they all had a vaguely familiar ring.

But what on earth were 'Tourentaeau Sampinon' (could they mean Tournedos Champignons?), 'cream rols', or 'stewed omons'? And could one really fancy 'roast lamb head', 'slring beans', or the 'chess board'?

Pride of place, however, went to something that must be a Greek speciality. It appeared under the heading 'roast', so presumably it referred to a main dish. Or perhaps it is the tourists who are being roasted in Greece, and what I took to be a dish is in fact a description of their feelings as they survey the bills at the end of their holiday. Either way, the words were simple yet descriptive: 'Bowels stuffed with spleen.'

But that little story, even though true, should not be taken as being too indicative of the state of Greek cooking. A few years ago it was common to read and hear quite savage attacks on the awfulness of Greek food, with travel experts advising holidaymakers to carry with them every medicament imaginable short of a stomach-pump. It is doubtful whether these criticisms were ever justified, and they are certainly not true today. Admittedly many Greek dishes are an acquired taste, and admittedly the only *taverna* to be found in some very remote parts may be, to say the least, somewhat basic. A diet of stale, oily meat and *retsina*, the resinated wine so beloved by Greeks, will play havoc with the hardiest constitution; but no doubt a Greek would be equally upset by an elderly pork pie and some greasy tea in a grubby roadside café in England. Eat wisely in Greece and you will eat well. Indeed, a meal will quickly become the prolonged pleasure that it is to almost every Greek.

The first secret of any Greek meal is not to be in a rush—because even if you are, the waiters won't be. Office hours in Greece are broken by a long siesta in the afternoon, so even a light lunch need not be a hurried affair. Businessmen work late, then join their friends or family for what is often the social highlight of the day: dinner. And whether they are eating at home, or in a restaurant or *taverna*, the Greeks like to sit long over their aperitifs (usually aniseed-flavoured *ouzo*, which turns cloudy when you add water or ice and is surprisingly strong) and then chat between courses. The men may even stand up and perform a lonely *syrtaki* dance when the mood takes them—it is bad manners to applaud such dancing, but tourists usually clap and will be forgiven for their ignorance.

At a party, or feast, the usual system is for the waiters to bring course after course to the table and for people to take whatever they want; at such meals appetites are always exhausted long before the menu is. In some very remote areas the old eastern-European and Middle-Eastern custom of eating from a communal pot still survives, although tourists are unlikely to come across it. What holidaymakers may find when eating with Greeks, however, is that they are offered a choice piece of meat or fruit from their companion's plate in the middle of the meal—a complimentary gesture that should not be refused. Equally, it is dangerous to slip into the childish habit of leaving 'the best bit' on your own plate until last—for your neighbour may well reach across and help himself!

But these idiosyncracies are rare. Usually you will have to contend with a menu which is in Greek and which may, therefore, be totally unintelligible to you, or with the habit—widely practised on the islands—where *taverna* customers walk into the kitchen to choose the main course. It is important to emphasize that no one will be surprised by such an act in Greece, and the state of the kitchen will do much to ease any remaining qualms you may have about Greek food, for every *taverna* kitchen I have ever seen has been spotless, even if it were cramped, hot and overcrowded.

If you want to be adventurous with your choice of food, then a peep into the kitchen will certainly aid your choice. But if not—what should you choose?

Two very safe choices are *souvlaki*, which is meat, usually lamb, grilled on a spit, and *moussaka*, a delicious pie containing minced meat and aubergine. Both are always made with fresh meat. A side salad, or *salata*, is usually ordered too, and this is a delicious affair sprinkled with olives and including *feta* as well as the more usual salad ingredients. Before the main course there are snacks known as *mezethes*, or very tasty *taramosalata*, a creamy paste made of fish roes and often eaten with hot bread.

In a country that lives so close to the sea, fish dishes are naturally common. Tiny red mullet (*barbounia*), grilled and eaten whole, are a tasty speciality, and sea bream (*lithinria*) are good too. Visitors should also ensure that they do not leave the country without tasting *kalamarakia*—crisply fried pieces of young squid. In the islands shellfish are popular, and a sort of *pilaff* is made of shrimps and prawns.

Other Greek favourites are *dolmathos*, stuffed vine leaves, served hot or cold, *avgolemono*, a lemon-flavoured chicken soup, and *youvarlakia*, boiled meat-balls with rice. Especially delicious, and a speciality of islands like Crete and Rhodes, are small, tasty cheese pies called *tyropitta*—eaten when they are freshly made and still hot. The hard *feta* goats' cheese, found all over the country, can be recommended—and of course there is fruit to follow, although your Greek companions may well choose sticky sweets instead. Many places also make their own yoghurt, which connoisseurs always rate highly.

The water is good almost everywhere, and there are also a number of local mineral-waters. Beer is more expensive than wine and some brands are not very good; but you may need it after a day in the hot sun, and if that is the case *Amstel* is the best—although the local *Fix* beer can now be found on draught and that, too, is good. With many areas producing their own wines, the choice can be bewildering in the best restaurants and non-existent in small country *tavernas*—but

Greek wines are, as a general rule, pleasantly light. ·Of the non-resinated wines, *Domestica*, from the Peloponnese, and the fuller-bodied *Naoussa* red wine from Macedonia, are popular. Although some people take to *retsina*—wine flavoured with resin to help it travel—right away, others can never acquire the taste; but it is something to try and restauranteurs or *taverna*-owners will be pleased to recommend a bottle without too much resin.

Although the various local wines, particularly those made on the islands, are often very good despite their 'home-made' taste, the same cannot always be said of the local brandies. Brandy drinkers should stick to *Metaxa*, and the seven-star *Gold Label Metaxa* at that, although even this is rough compared with its western-European counterparts.

Apart from the food, perhaps the greatest attraction of Greek *tavernas*, as well as some restaurants, is that they are also places of entertainment. There may be a resident band or singer, or in less sophisticated parts you may find simply a *bouzouki* player or even a waiter who every now and again stops serving and sings a song or two instead. And if there is no live entertainment, you may well find that the proprietor has made the best of a bad job and installed a jukebox. If that is the case, don't be put off; the records will all be Greek. Greek diners love a lot of noise.

Tavernas also have one other great factor in their favour: they will never turn you away. Once, when I stopped at a *taverna* in a quiet corner of Rhodes for a drink and decided to stay for an early lunch, the whole family got to work. The proprietor set the table and poured *ouzo*, his wife grilled fish, and a diminutive child was sent running for bread and *feta* cheese. If I had realized that I was, by Greek standards, too early for a meal I would never have put them to the inconvenience, but they would not hear of my leaving and insisted upon providing more drinks while I waited. The final bill: just a few pence. A similar thing happened in Corfu where the owner of an attractive little *taverna*'s only regret was that he could not persuade me to drink the thick Greek coffee, served in tiny cups that seem half full of sediment—an acquired taste that can be very refreshing if you remember to order it medium sweet, or *metrio*. For the faint-hearted, Nescafé is available all over Greece.

Shopping for souvenirs in the Greek islands is an adventure. There are some excellent bargains to be found, but both quality and prices vary from place to place. And don't bother with 'genuine' antiques or what look like classical pieces of art. Quite apart from the fact that exporting antiquities without a licence is forbidden, the Greeks have developed the faking of antiques into an art. There is the occasional medium-priced icon to be found, although this is more likely on the mainland. Modern reproductions are often convincing and attractive, but occasionally quite bad.

On the islands, handicrafts and other locally produced goods—sponges, for example—are relatively cheap, although the prices are inflated on the more popular islands like Mykonos. Corfu, the Ionian islands and Rhodes are the best places for jewellery, while the Ionian islands and the Cyclades also have the biggest (and cheapest) selection of embroidered clothing. There is good lace to be found on Rhodes and very attractive embroidered dresses on Santorini and Crete. Remember that you can still bargain over prices on the islands—it is expected on the smaller islands and the first price quoted will be given on the expectation that you will knock it down by at least one third. In the main tourist centres, however, the souvenir-shops and boutiques are changing over to the western-European practice of putting a price tag on things and turning up their noses at any offer which is below that figure.

Shoes—in leather, of course—are also very good value, and besides the holiday sandals which hang in clusters outside every souvenir-shop, women especially will find that more formal shoes of remarkably modern design can be bought very cheaply in the main shopping-areas of islands like Crete, Rhodes and Corfu. Some stores will even make shoes to measure for you at prices far below what you would pay for a quite ordinary pair at home.

Perhaps the best island for shopping is Rhodes, which—together with the rest of the Dodecanese group of islands—is a duty-free area. The price reductions to be found on Rhodes are really of benefit only to visiting Greeks buying imported goods, but the fact that the island is a duty-free resort has provided the impetus to change it into a major shopping-centre. Furs are surprisingly good value and of good quality.

A regrettable American and western-European practice, that of building shopping-arcades inside major hotels, has recently been introduced into Greece. These shops are excellent for browsing through and for purchasing newspapers, toilet requisites or other minor items, but like airport shops they are run on a concessionary basis and prices may be inflated. I have always found that I can do better outside in the town when making anything but a minor purchase.

Souvenir ideas to bring home from a holiday on the islands include woven and leather bags, other leather goods of all kinds, peasant-type blouses, embroidered dresses, pottery, brass-work, and coloured braid for dresses or other items of clothing. And, finally, nobody goes home without at least one set of *kombolia*, the brightly coloured worry-beads with which Greeks play interminably.

INDEX

INDEX